P A T I E N T
S A F E T Y

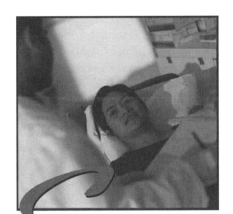
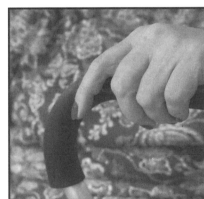
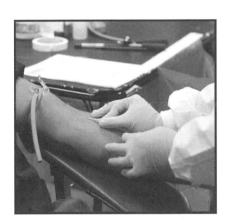

Essentials for Health Care

FOURTH EDITION

WITHDRAWN

Improving Health Care Quality and Safety

Part II: Safety Standards and the Accreditation Process

Introduction

The primary responsibility of health care organizations is to help individuals obtain or return to health and wellness. To do this, organizations and their staff must provide safe, appropriate care to the patients they serve.

The Joint Commission strongly believes that to ensure patient safety, organizations must establish a culture in which errors are proactively identified, staff can feel free to report incidents, and safety is rooted in the daily work of individual health care professionals and other staff. Some ways in which the Joint Commission has worked to help organizations create this culture of safety include the following:

- Setting state-of-the-art standards that focus on the quality and safety of health care

- Developing and implementing the Joint Commission's accreditation process

- Providing opportunities for consumer feedback through the Joint Commission's Office of Quality Monitoring

- Involving patients and families in health care through the Speak Up™ initiative

- Maintaining and mining the Sentinel Event Database

- Issuing *Sentinel Event Alert*

- Establishing and continuing the National Patient Safety Goals

- Establishing the Joint Commission International Center for Patient Safety

- Collaborating with the World Health Organization (WHO) to eliminate errors worldwide

- Partnering with the Institute for Healthcare Improvement on its 100,000 Lives Campaign

- Supporting safety-related legislative initiatives

- Serving as a convener, collaborator, educator, publisher, researcher, and so forth

Each of these initiatives is addressed in more detail in Chapter 1.

Content of the Book

This book offers a complete look at the Joint Commission's safety initiatives, including a comprehensive overview of the safety standards, the National Patient Safety Goals, and ways to prevent sentinel events. In addition, the book addresses topics such as proactive risk assessment, root cause analysis (RCA), and staffing effectiveness. Discussions involving how these topics relate to patient safety can be found throughout the publication.

Chapter 1, "Patient Safety: The Joint Commission Initiative," provides an overview of the Joint Commission's work to help organizations with their patient safety efforts. The chapter discusses safety as a key Joint Commission focus and identifies all the elements of the Joint Commission's safety initiative, including the safety standards and the accreditation process that accommodates an increased emphasis on safety. Additional topics include discussions on how organizations can conduct proactive risk assessment to prevent errors before they occur and how they can use RCA to conduct an analysis of sentinel events when they occur.

Chapter 2, "The Joint Commission's 2006 National Patient Safety Goals," discusses the 2006 program-specific goals and associated requirements including the changes and updates to the 2005 goals that are being carried over into 2006. This chapter also includes information on how the 2006 goals are surveyed and scored. In addition, this chapter provides a question-and-answer

PATIENT SAFETY Essentials for Health Care, Fourth Edition

PART I

Patient Safety: An Overview

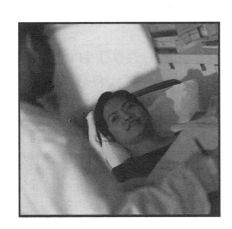 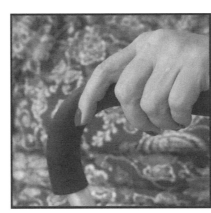 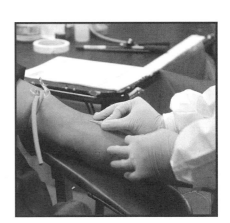

take time to implement, and the Joint Commission's survey data show that the 2005 goals were not fully implemented in all organizations (based on the most recent available data). As of January 1, 2006, all accredited organizations that provide care relevant to these goals and requirements are expected to be in compliance with the 2006 goals and requirements. More information on the goals is presented in Chapter 2.

- Providing opportunities for consumer feedback. The Joint Commission's Office of Quality Monitoring (OQM) receives, evaluates, tracks, and responds to complaints and reports of concerns about health care organizations from patients, families, staff, and the public, and acts on complaints when necessary.

- Supporting safety-related legislative initiatives. For many years, the Joint Commission has advised Congress and has worked with state legislatures to develop initiatives to address patient safety and medical errors, as well as to develop sentinel event reporting systems.

In addition, the Joint Commission demonstrates its commitment to safety by involving patients and families in their health care through its SpeakUp™ campaign; by informing the public about an accredited health care organization's safety efforts through Quality Reports posted online at Quality Check® (http://www.qualitycheck.org); through Public Policy Initiatives relating to patient safety (*see* pages 25–27 for more information); through research (such as the development of the patient safety taxonomy and patient safety indicators); and through collaborations, education programs, and publications.

The Joint Commission provides its health care accreditation standards and processes in support of quality and safety efforts. Specifically, the safety and error reduction standards provide a framework for helping to reduce the risk to and ensure the safety of individuals who receive care, treatment, and services in health care organizations. At its heart, accreditation is a risk-reduction activity; compliance with standards is intended to reduce the risk of adverse outcomes.

In recent years, more public attention has

been focused on safety issues in health care facilities. The Joint Commission has a shared vision with health care organizations as well as with health care oversight bodies and the public to bridge what has been called a gap or chasm between the current state of health care and the potential for safer, higher-quality care.

Patient Safety–Related Standards

One of the key elements in the Joint Commission's commitment to patient safety is the expansion of safety-related standards. Based on the Joint Commission's experience with sentinel event monitoring, as well as the opinions of health care experts, leaders, and accredited organizations, the standards advocate a shift toward an environment in which actual and potential risks are identified to prevent or minimize the number and severity of adverse outcomes (such as sentinel events). The safety standards address requirements for an organizationwide patient safety program and stress the importance of overall patient safety. Although safety and risk management have always been addressed in the standards, the changes put these issues at the forefront of leadership, staff, and patient/family awareness. Ensuring patient safety and reducing the risk of negative outcomes to patients are not new concepts and are probably already built into most organization activities. The safety standards simply help focus attention on these areas and add some new tools for improving patient safety.

A Focus on Leadership

The safety standards appear in several areas of the Joint Commission's accreditation manuals, but the strongest focus is on leaders' responsibility to build an environment that recognizes the importance of safety. Acknowledging that effective error reduction requires an integrated and coordinated approach, the Joint Commission's "Leadership" (LD) standards describe leaders' roles in an organizationwide safety program. In general, the LD standards require leaders to do the following:

- Encourage decision making as a collaborative activity. Leaders must foster communication and cooperation among individuals and departments to implement ways to improve patient safety.

- Implement an integrated patient safety program throughout the organization. Components should include staffing the program; a description of the program's scope of activities; methods to ensure participation of all areas of the organization; procedures for proactive risk assessment and risk reduction; procedures for response to errors and other adverse occurrences; reporting systems; and an annual report to the governing body.

- Ensure processes are designed well, using available information from internal or external sources about potential risks to patients and successful practices

- Adequately allocate human, information, time, physical, and financial resources to support identified performance and patient safety improvement activities

- Measure and assess leadership contributions to performance and patient safety improvements to ensure that they are effective

Performance Improvement

The Joint Commission's "Improving Organization Performance" (PI) standards outline how health care organizations can ensure that they design processes well and systematically monitor, analyze, and improve their performance to improve care, treatment, and service outcomes. Standards revisions build on requirements from the LD chapter and cover the following areas:

- Establishment of an ongoing, proactive program to identify safety risks and reduce errors

- Consideration of the organization's history of unanticipated adverse events in prioritizing opportunities for improvement during the planning process and consideration of patient safety issues when designing and redesigning processes

- Collection of data specifically relating to patient, family, and staff opinions and perceptions of risk, suggestions for improvement, and staff willingness to report errors to monitor performance

- Performance with undesirable patterns and sentinel events should be intensively analyzed

- Intensive analysis of undesirable patterns and sentinel events

- Identification, through data collection, of changes leading to improved performance and patient safety

Other Functions

Leadership and performance improvement are not the only functions that house the safety standards. A safety standard within the "Ethics, Rights, and Responsibilities" (RI) chapter requires patients and their families to be educated about their roles in reporting perceived risks to patient care. A licensed independent practitioner or other caregiver responsible for a patient's care should explain all outcomes, including any unexpected outcomes of care, to the patient/family. Within the "Management of Human Resources" (HR) function, the standards require staff orientation, ongoing in services/continuing education, and team training to emphasize specific safety-related aspects of each job. In addition, "Management of Information" (IM) standards require systems to collect and aggregate any data that are necessary to support risk reduction and emphasize the importance of effective communication in protecting patients from harm.

Because health care encompasses so many diverse settings, not all safety standards will be applicable to all settings. As organizations review the standards, they will notice how specific standards fit within their current processes and procedures. While this chapter introduces several components of the safety standards, specific requirements are presented in Chapter 3.

Culture of Safety

An organization cannot truly improve patient safety if it waits for sentinel events to occur before taking action to address system issues. The approaches most commonly used in the past and those easiest to implement—punitive actions and retraining or counseling—have proven least effective in producing successful, long-term results. Cultural change, technical system

Proactive Risk Reduction

Many organizations struggle with the how-tos of taking a proactive approach to improving safety and preventing errors. One way to facilitate proactive error reduction is to establish a small group of staff members that reviews reports about potential safety issues and proactively explores whether an opportunity exists to improve processes or systems. Such a group might include clinical analysts, nurse executives, legal representatives, pharmacists, and representatives from the chief-of-staff's office, risk management, and performance improvement. The group should meet regularly to review information from traditional incident reports as well as from informal reports, thus seizing the opportunity to intervene before someone is harmed.

Creating a culture of safety is not easy, and it does take time. Sidebar 1-2 above offers tips for successfully creating such a culture.

Creating a Patient Safety Program

A commitment to patient safety within a health care organization requires a clearly defined, coordinated, and ongoing patient safety program. Putting together such an organizationwide program requires a lot of planning, organizing, and refining. Some organizations have most of the required activities and processes in place (for example, risk management, performance improvement, environmental safety, infection control) and need only to integrate them with a safety-related focus. Others may look at all the components that need to be coordinated and wonder where to start.

The first step in compliance is to review all organization functions affected by the standards and make sure that the requirements relating to those functions are understood.

Developing the Structure

Although not required by Joint Commission standards, some health care organizations establish a structure or framework for patient safety that will ensure visible organization commitment and attention to patient safety goals and standards. Organizations have many options for developing such a structure, including the following:

1. Develop a patient safety committee that monitors all safety efforts throughout the organization

2. Integrate the patient safety–related efforts of various existing committees within a coordinating council

3. Expand the scope of current committee responsibilities and accountability to include patient safety

4. Assign one person to coordinate patient safety initiatives in various areas

These choices come down to two main options:

1. Keeping patient safety as a part of current committees/functions and implementing a focal point for coordination and accountability

Or

2. Creating a new structure devoted entirely to integrating and coordinating patient safety efforts

Whether an organization chooses to create a new structure or to work within an existing one, the choice is open and should be made based on the organization's size, current structures, strengths, preferences, and a careful evaluation of alternatives.

Sidebar 1-3, at right, summarizes the key components of a patient safety program.

Key Steps in Creating a Written Patient Safety Plan

Developing a comprehensive patient safety program can be a daunting task. It may be helpful to write a formalized plan outlining the details of such a program. The following sections discuss components of a written plan that can help organizations organize and keep track of safety program elements. Although Joint Commission standards address the implementation of a safety program, they do not require a written plan. Nor is it helpful to develop documentation just for the sake of documentation. However, in this case, many organizations find it helpful to have a written plan that facilitates education, communication, consistency, and effectiveness.

The basic building blocks of a written safety plan include the following:

- The scope of the plan (that is, what processes are involved)

- Measurable goals of the plan

- Accountability for achieving those goals

- Channels of communication that will allow information about the plan to be shared

Defining the Scope. Identifying what processes and activities affect patient safety is important because a safety program is not a separate entity but is woven through the many functions performed in an organization. To clearly identify all areas affected by patient safety efforts, some organizations list existing activities in the organization that relate to patient safety. These activities may

---

> ### Sidebar 1-3. Key Components of a Patient Safety Program
>
> A patient safety program does the following:
>
> - Designates one or more qualified individuals or an inter-disciplinary group to manage the organizationwide patient safety program
>
> - Defines the scope of its activities—that is, the types of occurrences to be addressed
>
> - Describes mechanisms to ensure that all components of the organization are integrated into and participate in the organizationwide program
>
> - Includes procedures for immediate response to system or process failures, including care of the affected patient(s), containment of risk to others, and preservation of factual information for subsequent analysis
>
> - Includes clear systems for internal and external reporting of information about system or process failures
>
> - Defines mechanisms for responding to the various types of occurrences, such as root cause analysis in response to a sentinel event, and for conducting proactive risk reduction activities
>
> - Defines mechanisms for support of staff members who have been involved in a sentinel event
>
> - At least annually, reports to the governing body on the occurrence of system or process failures and actions taken to improve patient safety, both proactively and in response to actual occurrences

---

occur within performance improvement, infection control, facilities/environmental management, and risk management programs, among others. This type of organizational assessment allows leaders to compare current safety activities with the functions outlined in the patient safety standards and identifies any holes.

In addition to an assessment, data collected through PI activities may be used by organizations to spot potential problems. In fact, data collection systems can be modified to include patient safety needs without duplicating effort.

Setting Program Goals. Once areas involving patient safety are identified, a section of the safety plan should describe how the various activities will be integrated and coordinated, and how the various activities will be coordinated with other functions. This section allows different staff members to see how their areas are involved and how the program works toward the organization's overall goals.

Stating the program's goals in the plan

errors, establish or enhance an error/near miss reporting mechanism, and identify a data collection plan and reporting structure and schedule. Reports to the governing board should include results and recommendations in a coordinated fashion.

The committee will likely tackle such activities as proactive risk reduction, team training, orientation to the safety-related aspects of each job, and disclosure of unexpected outcomes of care to patients and families. Organization leaders should choose relatively simple projects to ease the committee into its work; early wins help to build trust between staff and administrators and enhance the group's ability to tackle larger, more complex issues.

The Joint Commission's Accreditation Process

The Joint Commission's accreditation process focuses on systems critical to safety and the quality of care, treatment, and services. Representing a shift in focus from survey preparation to continuous standards compliance and operational improvement, this process encourages organizations to incorporate the standards as a guide for routine operations. The process is designed to follow more naturally how an organization provides care, treatment, and services to its patients. For instance, rather than include activities created just for survey, the survey runs tandem with an organization's normal systems. As a result, public confidence that health care organizations continuously comply with standards that emphasize patient safety and health care quality should increase.

The Joint Commission's accreditation process comprises a variety of elements, each of which is discussed in greater detail in Chapter 5.

Physician Engagement in Accreditation and Safety

As part of its accreditation process, the Joint Commission has worked to enhance the relevance of accreditation to physicians by better engaging them in the accreditation process and by helping them to provide safe, high-quality care. Few would disagree that physicians are critical to patient safety. They serve in leadership roles in health care organizations through their responsibility for directing the creation of a patient care plan and its follow-through. Their involvement is essential to the success of patient safety initiatives aimed at reducing sentinel events and avoiding system failures at the root of these occurrences. Because of this, physicians must be involved in the development and implementation of organizational patient safety initiatives.

All too often, however, time and workload constraints make it challenging for physicians to participate in an organization's safety initiatives. Health care organizations and physicians struggle with the tension created by these constraints. Both parties desire high-quality care outcomes and patient safety. Consequently, both parties must make the time commitment. Patient safety cannot be an "extra" activity; instead, it should be a driving force of the medical profession. Following are tips for encouraging physician engagement in accreditation and safety.

- Implement a culture of safety. Health care leaders must ensure an environment and culture conducive to communication and collaboration, and physicians must be a part of that leadership effort. Physicians' collaboration as integral members of multidisciplinary teams is essential to the way care is provided. Physicians should participate in organizationwide performance improvement teams to investigate the root causes of medical failures that have occurred and proactively work to identify and implement failure reduction opportunities. Some physicians express concern about the time involved in such endeavors, worried that they take time away from direct patient care. Yet because patient care is physicians' first priority, their involvement in these safety-related efforts is critical and must be considered part of the care they provide. Health care leaders need to ensure that physicians can optimize their time while remaining engaged in patient safety initiatives. Activities should be streamlined whenever possible. Use of voice mail and e-mail can keep physicians informed of team discussions. Meetings should have agendas and begin and end on time. Physician attendance only during key decision-making meetings can be explored, as can other strategies to make the best use of their time.

- Focus on initiatives that offer technological solutions. When designed and used properly, technology can increase efficiency and aid a practitioner's quest for improved patient safety. Technological solutions that reduce the likelihood of medical failures have been particularly impressive in the realm of medication use processes. For example, CPOE, or "electronic prescribing," can eliminate many problems associated with prescribing, including handwriting and transcription errors. It can also ensure that dosage, form, and frequency are appropriate and perform a check for potential drug-drug interactions.

- Improve staff communication. The need for improved and increased communication by and among physicians and other health care professionals warrants special focus. Communication failures were cited in 66% of all sentinel events that have been reviewed by the Joint Commission since 1995, making this problem the most frequently occurring problem associated with all types of sentinel events. When seeking physician support, organizations should keep in mind the following points regarding improved communication:

  - Leaders can help improve communication with physicians by providing concise information about an initiative's expected effect on care quality and safety. Communication must be quantitative and practical. Quantification and communication of what might occur if the organization does not undertake the initiative can be compelling (for example, "x number of" serious medication errors could occur each day, with possible effects including injury and death).

  - Communication failures must be viewed as having systems roots rather than as attributable to any specific health care professional. Physicians do not act alone, yet some individuals might be apprehensive about whether safety initiatives are designed to identify and punish "outliers." Organizationwide communication about safety initiatives must focus on a realization that system improvement is something beyond just individual performance.

- To be appropriately involved in safety initiatives, health care professionals must communicate with their colleagues as true team members. Many, but not all, physicians understand the dangers of a hierarchical culture in which health care staff perform autonomously. However, to have successful team communication, physicians must buy in to the benefits of enhanced teamwork, collaboration, and communication. Physicians are most likely to be receptive to team participation when it is championed by another physician. It is important to find physicians who acknowledge the initiative's purpose and scope.

- Physicians are often hesitant to join team initiatives because of the perceived time commitment. Clear specification of the time likely to be required helps physicians make an informed decision about participation. Perceptions of what might be required can greatly exceed the actual time commitment.

- Develop strong physician-patient communication. In addition to communication among physicians and other health care professionals, communication among physicians and patients and their families is essential to quality medical care and improved patient safety. The patient should be a partner to the physician in the care process both when things are going well and when they are not going as well as expected. Patients and family members must also be educated about the value of increased communication with care providers. The Joint Commission's Speak Up™ campaign encourages patients and families to inform caregivers if they have questions or concerns about some aspect of care. (*See* Sidebar 1-4, Strategies for Enhancing Physician-to-Physician and Staff-to-Physician Communication, page 19, for more information on improving communication.)

In addition, the Joint Commission recently established an 18-member Physician Engagement Advisory Group, which will advise the Joint Commission in its efforts to expand physician participation in the accreditation process and broaden physician engagement in quality of care and patient safety initiatives.

Failure Mode and Effects Analysis

One approach to proactive risk assessment is failure mode and effects analysis (FMEA). Although the Joint Commission does not require organizations to conduct FMEA, it is one way organizations can anticipate problems and put systems in place to prevent adverse outcomes and ultimately enhance patient safety.

FMEA can be effective when used alone, but it is even more effective when it is used as part of an ongoing comprehensive quality management or performance improvement process. Such a process provides the data and information needed to accurately identify real or potential failure modes and improvement opportunities. It also ensures the documentation of procedures, which is critical to measuring and reducing the variation in performance of the procedure(s). FMEA explores how procedures are performed and how they might be better performed to reduce the likelihood of error.

Root Cause Analysis

While proactive risk assessment is an important tool available to prospectively examine ways that failures can occur in health care processes, root cause analysis (RCA) is a tool for examining a process retrospectively once an adverse event has occurred. RCA can also be used to probe a "near miss" or "close call"—a problem that almost occurred—or even a potential failure mode identified in a proactive risk assessment.

The Joint Commission's Sentinel Event Policy requires organizations to perform an RCA after the occurrence of a sentinel event, thus helping organizations discover the true issues behind a problem. RCA identifies the basic causal factors that underlie variation in performance. It is then used to identify opportunities for improvement that will prevent recurrence. A root cause is the most fundamental reason(s) for the occurrence of a situation in which performance does not meet expectations.

RCA focuses primarily on systems and processes, not on individual performance. It can do more than determine that *A* caused *B*. The process can also help an organization

see that "if we change *A*, we can reduce the possibility of *B* recurring or in fact prevent *B* from occurring in the first place."

The RCA process should identify potential improvements in processes or systems that would likely decrease the occurrence of adverse events in the future. In some (rare) cases, the analysis might indicate that no such improvement opportunities exist. The product of an RCA is an action plan that identifies strategies that the organization can implement to reduce the risk of similar events.

Questions that should be addressed within a root cause analysis include the following:

- What might be the causes of a problem?

- Might the causes be the result of human resources issues, information management issues, environmental management issues, or leadership and communication issues, among others?

RCA and FMEA: How They Interrelate

Root cause analysis and failure mode and effects analysis have many similarities and differences. While RCA is primarily a reactive approach to systems analysis, FMEA is primarily a proactive approach to the prevention of systems-related failures. RCA asks "Why?" after an event has occurred, probing for underlying root causes of an event. FMEA asks "What if?" FMEA explores what could happen if a failure occurred at a particular step in a process or in a link between steps.

Both RCA and FMEA are important tools for preventing errors in high-risk health care processes. Both are key to performance improvement. RCA and FMEA share the following characteristics:

- Both are nonstatistical methods of analysis

- Both have the goal of reducing the possibility of future patient harm

- Both involve identifying conditions that lead to harm

- Both are team activities

Table 1-1, on page 21, presents the two approaches' most marked differences. Yet an organization can benefit when it conducts both RCA and FMEA. In fact, the two approaches can be used in conjunction with each other. For example, one RCA step involves evaluating possible improvement actions. This step occurs late in the process after root causes of an event have been identified. The RCA team compiles a list of possible improvement actions which is as complete as possible. Members of the RCA team must then evaluate the alternatives to select the actions that are most worthy of implementation. At this point, FMEA can be a helpful tool because it involves evaluating problems (that could result from proposed improvement actions) and prioritizing or ranking them according to criteria defined by the team. By using FMEA at this point, the team can identify what might go wrong with a redesigned process and identify any new failure modes that might have been introduced as a result of a process redesign.

One way to use RCA in FMEA involves identifying the root causes of failure modes. This step occurs after the team has fully studied the high risk process, brainstormed potential failure modes, and prioritized the failure modes. An RCA approach can be used at this point in the FMEA process to determine the systemic roots of a potential problem.

While RCA is helpful here, a full RCA is not required. Rather, the objective is to identify some actionable items that would prevent critical failures. In essence, identifying actionable items that would prevent critical failures represents a prospective use of RCA.

Why Use Both Processes?

The Joint Commission requires use of both RCA and a proactive risk assessment process (such as FMEA) as part of an organization's comprehensive performance improvement process. Analyzing processes *after* a sentinel event or near miss occurs (RCA) must be joined with a prospective look at what could go wrong *before* a sentinel event occurs (FMEA or a similar proactive process). If organizations do not approach performance improvement using both methods, they will constantly jump from one retrospective analysis to another, responding to events as they occur rather than prospectively designing or redesigning processes to prevent adverse outcomes. In the real world, both RCA and FMEA are recommended tools for every organization's toolkit.

Table 1-1. Differences Between RCA and FMEA	
Root Cause Analysis	**Failure Mode and Effects Analysis**
Reactive	Proactive
Focuses on a single event (typically)	Focuses on entire process
Hindsight bias	Unbiased
Asks "Why?"	Asks "What if?"

Other Components of the Joint Commission's Safety Initiative

Developing the safety standards, revising the accreditation process, and encouraging proactive risk assessment are some of the approaches the Joint Commission is using to improve patient safety across organizations. In addition, the Joint Commission has been approaching the safety initiative through other channels, including a complaint hotline and actively participating in legislative initiatives involving patient safety.

The Office of Quality Monitoring

The Joint Commission's Office of Quality Monitoring (OQM) receives, evaluates, and tracks complaints and reports of concerns about health care organizations regarding quality-of-care issues. Information often comes from patients, their families, or the public, as well as from an organization's own staff, government agencies, and other sources. The OQM has a toll-free hotline, 800/994-6610, and also receives written reports by mail or e-mail. When a report is submitted, the Joint Commission reviews any past reports and the organization's most recent accreditation decision. Depending on the nature of the reported concern, the Joint Commission will take one of the following actions:

- Incorporate the reported concern into the quality monitoring database that is used to track health care organizations over time to identify trends or patterns in their performance

- Ask the organization to provide a written response to the reported concern

- Review the reported concern and compliance with related standards at the time of the organization's next accreditation survey

complications of surgery occur in 2% to 5% of patients undergoing noncardiac surgery and as many as 34% of patients undergoing vascular surgery. Certain perioperative cardiac events, such as myocardial infarction, are associated with a mortality rate of 40% to 70% per event, prolonged hospitalization, and higher costs. Current studies suggest that appropriately administered beta-blockers reduce perioperative ischemia, especially in patients considered to be at risk. Nearly half of the fatal cardiac events could be prevented with beta-blocker therapy.

3. Deep vein thrombosis (DVT): DVT occurs after approximately 25% of all major surgical procedures performed without prophylaxis, and pulmonary embolism (PE) in 7% of surgeries conducted without prophylaxis. More than 50% of major orthopedic procedures are complicated by DVT, and up to 30% by PE, if prophylactic treatment is not instituted. Despite the well-established efficacy and safety of preventive measures, studies show that prophylaxis is often underused or used inappropriately.

4. Postoperative pneumonia: According to the CDC, this condition has been associated with high fatality rates. Postoperative pneumonia occurs in 9% to 40% of patients and has an associated mortality rate of 30% to 46%. Many of the factors respond amenably to medical intervention and thus are preventable. A conservative estimate of the potential savings of the reduced hospitalization due to postoperative pneumonia is $22,000 to $28,000 per patient per admission.

Each of SCIP's four target areas is advised by a TEP. These groups have provided hours of technical expertise and resources to ensure the SCIP measures are fully supported by evidence-based research.

SCIP is one of the first national quality improvement initiatives to unite national hospital, physician, and nursing organizations; the federal government; the Joint Commission; and private sector experts in far-reaching quality improvement and patient safety efforts.

SCIP focuses on process measures, such as the appropriate use of antibiotics near the time of surgery and the use of beta blockers to prevent cardiovascular events.

The Joint Commission is working with CMS to align and merge the SCIP and ICU measures for incorporation in the Specifications Manual for National Hospital Quality Measures.

Legislative Efforts

The Joint Commission believes that it is necessary to create a nonpunitive environment in which health care errors and patient safety information can be reported. The Joint Commission has advised Congress on the need for federal statutory protection of reported information—especially RCA information—and has sought legislation that will facilitate the study and reporting of health care error information and adequately protect that information from disclosure in civil law suits.

In 2005 Joint Commission President Dennis S. O'Leary, M.D., testified before the Health Subcommittee of the House Energy and Commerce Committee regarding the need for health care facilities to embrace a "systems approach" to preventing adverse events that keeps the inevitable errors that caregivers make from reaching patients. In his testimony, Dr. O'Leary underscored the fact that health care must create an environment in which safety is always top of mind and errors are viewed as opportunities for learning and improvement. A systems approach can mitigate the effects of mistakes by designing systems that anticipate human error and prevent the occurrence of adverse events. Dr. O'Leary also commented that the very nature of health care requires continuing vigilance to identify emerging patient safety risks.

In addition, the Joint Commission has supported the enactment of federal patient safety legislation that will encourage the voluntary reporting of medical errors, serious adverse events, and their underlying causes. The Patient Safety and Quality Improvement Act of 2005, signed by President George W. Bush in July 2005, will promote cultures of safety across health care settings by establishing federal protections that encourage thorough, candid examinations of the causes of health care errors and the development of effective solutions to prevent their recurrence. Previously, evaluative information about the underlying causes of adverse events was not always considered confidential or protected from lawsuits, a fact that the Institute of Medicine blamed for driving errors underground and slowing progress in improving patient safety.

The Patient Safety and Quality Improvement Act of 2005 provides full federal privilege to patient safety information that is transmitted to a Patient Safety Organization. The Joint Commission expects to create or become part of a Patient Safety Organization under the auspices of its new International Center for Patient Safety (*see* page 22) and seek federal approval under a new process to be created by the Department of Health and Human Services.

On the state level, the Joint Commission is pursuing collaborative agreements with states that have mandatory sentinel event reporting systems as well as those that do not currently require reporting.

Speak Up™

The Speak Up™ program, launched by the Joint Commission and the Centers for Medicare & Medicaid Services (CMS), is a national campaign designed to reduce errors by increasing patient involvement in their own care. It encourages patients to become active, involved, and informed participants of the health care team. CMS supports such efforts to increase consumer awareness and involvement.

The Speak Up™ program urges patients to do the following:

- **S**peak up if you have questions or concerns, and if you don't understand, ask again. It's your body and you have a right to know.

- **P**ay attention to the care you are receiving. Make sure you're getting the right treatments and medications by the right health care professionals. Don't assume anything.

- **E**ducate yourself about your diagnosis, the medical tests you are undergoing, and your treatment plan.

- **A**sk a trusted family member or friend to be your advocate.

- **K**now what medications you take and why you take them. Medication errors are the most common health care errors.

- **U**se a hospital, clinic, surgery center, or other type of health care organization that has undergone a rigorous on-site evaluation against established state-of-the-art quality and safety standards, such as that provided by the Joint Commission.

- **P**articipate in all decisions about your treatment. You are the center of the health care team.

Note: *This language is slightly different for each accreditation program.*

Other Speak Up™ initiatives include the following:

- Help Prevent Errors in Your Care: For Surgical Patients

- Preparing to be a Living Organ Donor

- Three Things You Can Do To Prevent Infection

- Universal Protocol for Preventing Wrong Site, Wrong Procedure, Wrong Person Surgery™

- Tips to Prevent Medications Mistakes

- Planning Your Recovery

- What You Should Know About Research Studies

Additional information about each of these initiatives is available at http://www.jointcommission.org.

Public Policy Initiatives

The Joint Commission has launched a series of public policy initiatives to identify achievable solutions to critical issues affecting the quality and safety of health care. The Joint Commission brings together health care experts to discuss issues that are of greatest concern to health care leaders and workers to identify workable solutions and assign specific accountabilities for action.

The Joint Commission's public policy action plan, identified as a strategic priority by its Board of Commissioners, focuses on key areas related to patient safety and health

PATIENT SAFETY Essentials for Health Care, Fourth Edition

CHAPTER 2

The Joint Commission's 2006 National Patient Safety Goals

The most difficult situation an organization can face is a sentinel event. Sentinel events occur when they are least expected and constitute the most significant lapse in patient safety that an organization can experience. The good news is that most sentinel events are preventable.

The Joint Commission has worked diligently with organizations on ways to anticipate and avoid sentinel events. One such venture is the National Patient Safety Goals—topics with requirements that relate to potential sentinel events and identify specific interventions to help organizations improve the safety of patient care.

The Sentinel Event Advisory Group, a Joint Commission–appointed, multidisciplinary group of experienced physicians, nurses, pharmacists, systems engineers, and other patient safety experts, has conducted thorough reviews of all *Sentinel Event Alert* recommendations and identified those that are candidates for inclusion in the National Patient Safety Goals. The Advisory Group does the following:

- Assesses the evidence for and validity of each past and proposed *Sentinel Event Alert* recommendation

- Reaches consensus on recommendations determined to be expert- or evidence-based

- Examines the practicality and cost-effectiveness of implementing each recommendation

- Recommends topics for future review and publication in *Sentinel Event Alert*

- Annually recommends National Patient Safety Goals to the Joint Commission's Board of Commissioners

- Advises the Joint Commission on the acceptability of alternative approaches to the goals and requirements

The 2006 goals, recommended by the Sentinel Event Advisory Group and approved by the Joint Commission's Board of Commissioners, include most goals and requirements from previous years. The 2006 goals are program specific and apply (as indicated) to ambulatory care (including ambulatory surgery centers), office-based surgery, behavioral health care, critical access hospitals, home care, hospitals, laboratories, long term care, disease-specific care, assisted living*, integrated delivery systems*, managed care organizations*, and preferred provider organizations.* The Joint Commission made the National Patient Safety Goals program-specific to increase the relevance of the goals and requirements to the individuals served in each program.

Beginning January 1, 2006, all accredited organizations that provide care relevant to these goals and requirements will be expected to comply with them. Compliance with all National Patient Safety Goals and requirements that are relevant to an organization's services will be evaluated for continuous compliance throughout the accreditation cycle through on-site surveys, the Periodic Performance Review (PPR)[†], and Evidence of Standards Compliance (ESC). Surveyors will look for evidence of consistent implementation of the requirements. Regardless of when a survey is conducted during the year, scoring will be based on an expectation of continued compliance since January 1, 2006 for requirements that are new in 2006 or for at least the preceding

---

* The Joint Commission has discontinued its assisted living, integrated delivery system, managed care organization, and preferred provider organization accreditation programs effective January 1, 2006. However, the Joint Commission will continue to provide a full array of support services and oversight to organizations accredited under these programs through the end of each organization's respective accreditation award period. No new accreditation surveys or resurveys under this program will be conducted.

† For programs required to complete the PPR.

Table 2-1. Program-Specific Retired and New National Patient Safety Goals for 2006

	AMB	ALF	BHC	CAH/HAP	DSC	LAB	LTC	OBS	OME	MCO/IDS/PPO
Goal 1A Patient IDs	X	X	X	X	X	X	X	X	X	N/A
Goal 1B time out	N/A	X	N/A	N/A	X	X	X	N/A	X	N/A
Goal 2A read back	X	X	X	X	X	X	X	X	X	N/A
Goal 2B abbrev	X	X	X	X	X	X	X	X	X	N/A
Goal 2C timely test report	X	N/A	X	X	X	X	N/A	X	X	N/A
Goal 2D Lab timely report	N/A	N/A	N/A	N/A	N/A	X	N/A	N/A	N/A	N/A
Goal 2E handoff	N	N	N	N	N	N	N	N	N	N/A
Goal 3A electrolytes	R	N/A	N/A	R	R	N/A	R	R	R	N/A
Goal 3B standard/limit con	X	N/A	X	X	X	N/A	X	X	X	N/A
Goal 3C Look/sound meds	X	N/A	X	X	N/A	N/A	X	X	X	N/A
Goal 3D labels	N	N/A	N/A	N	N/A	N/A	N/A	N	N/A	N/A
Goal 4A wrong patient surgery	N/A	N/A	N/A	N/A	X	N/A	N/A	N/A	N/A	N/A
Goal 5A infusion	R	R	R	R	R	N/A	R	R	R	N/A
Goal 6A/B alarms	N/A	N/A	N/A	N/A	X	N/A	N/A	N/A	N/A	N/A
Goal 7A/B hand hygiene	X	X	X	X	X	X	X	X	X	N/A
Goal 8A/B reconcile meds	X	X	X	X	X	N/A	X	X	X	N/A
Goal 9A assess for falls	N/A	R	N/A	R	N/A	N/A	R	N/A	R	N/A
Goal 9B fall reduction program	N/A	N*	N/A	N*	N	N/A	X	N/A	N*	N/A
Goal 10A/B/C influenza	N/A	X	N/A	N/A	X	N/A	X	N/A	N/A	N/A
Goal 11A surgical fires	X	N/A	N/A	N/A	N/A	N/A	N/A	X	N/A	N/A
Goal 12A MCO/IDS/PPO	N/A	N/A	N/A	N/A	N/A	N/A	N/A	N/A	N/A	X
Goal 13A patient involvement	N/A	N	N/A	N/A	N	N	N/A	N/A	N	N/A
Goal 14A pressure ulcer	N/A	N/A	N/A	N/A	N/A	N/A	N	N/A	N/A	N/A
Universal Protocol	X	N/A	N/A	X	N/A	N/A	N/A	X	N/A	N/A

* AMB, ambulatory care; ALF, assisted living facility; BHC, behavioral health care; CAH, critical access hospital; HAP, hospital; DSC, disease-specific care; LAB, laboratory; LTC, long term care; OBS, office-based surgery; OME, home care; MCO, managed care organization; IDS, integrated delivery system; PPO, preferred provider organization.

X = Applicable in 2005 and 2006   R = Retired for 2006
N = New for 2006   N* = Goal 9B actually replaces Goal 9A
N/A = Does not apply in 2005 or in 2006

patient (the name and the unique number would be the two pieces of information).

All organizations must comply with this goal regardless of whether their laboratory is accredited by the Joint Commission. Nonlaboratory staff members must also comply with this goal if they are taking samples on behalf of the laboratory.

Compliance Solutions

Organizations can use information such as the patient's name, an assigned ID number, the patient's birth date, or bar coding that includes two or more patient-specific identifiers (*not* the patient's room or bed number) as identifiers, but the same two identifiers do not have to be used throughout the organization. Different identifiers may be used in different settings, as long as their use is consistent with the intent of this requirement. However, the identifiers should be consistent within each setting, not just whatever the individual practitioner or staff person wishes to use.

For example, one organization's laboratory department added an additional four-digit number to the ID band when taking blood samples. The laboratory will not accept any blood samples if the two patient identifier documentation does not include the unique four-digit number. The unique number can only be found on the patient's ID band, which ensures that the patient's ID has at least been checked.

When verifying the name with the patient, staff should never state the name and ask the patient to confirm it. Confused patients or individuals in a behavioral health care setting might agree even when it is not their name. Safer practice is to ask the patient to state his or her own name. Some organizations have patients verify their own identity. Having patients verify their own identity is appropriate as long as staff consider the patient reliable enough to do so. Following are some setting-specific tips for complying with this requirement:

- *Ambulatory care.* Make sure the room, bed, cubicle, or bay number is not used as one of the identifiers for Goal 1A.

- *Behavioral health care.* Goal 1A does not apply to self-administered medication or psychosocial interventions. For long-stay programs, such as group homes, direct facial recognition is only appropriate when the staff and client population are both stable.

- *Home care.* In any situation of continuing one-on-one care in which the nurse "knows" the individual (there is an established nurse-to-patient relationship), for Goal 1A, one of the identifiers can be direct facial recognition. In the home, the correct address (an acceptable identifier when used in conjunction with another person-specific identifier) can also be confirmed, as can the patient's Social Security number or driver's license number.

- *Long term care settings.* For cognitively impaired residents, the staff might use a photograph in the clinical record to serve as visual identification. Direct facial recognition of residents is acceptable when the staff and resident population are stable. For long-stay residents, the photograph must be updated.

- *Laboratory.* It is expected that all specimens come to the laboratory with a minimum of two identifiers on them, however, laboratories should not reject specimens that arrive without two identifiers because some samples are irretrievable, expensive to recollect, or will cause a treatment delay if recollected. Laboratories should establish written guidelines for specimen rejection and should include a cautionary statement on the laboratory report indicating the specimen was received in the laboratory without complete identification.

Requirement 1B: Prior to the start of any invasive procedure, conduct a final verification process[*] to confirm the correct patient or resident, procedure, site, and availability of appropriate documents.[†] This verification process uses active—not passive—communication techniques. (Applicable to assisted living, disease-specific care, home care, long term care)

Requirement 1B: Immediately prior to the start of any invasive procedure, conduct a

---

[*] Add "such as a 'time out'" for **home care, long term care,** and **assisted living**.

[†] Remove "availability of appropriate documents" for **home care, long term care, and assisted living.**

duration and can highlight potential duplicative therapies from different practitioners. Including this information can also minimize the potential confusion of look-alike and sound-alike medications. The order must also include the drug name, the dosage form, the strength or concentration, the frequency, the route, the quantity, and the duration. Organizations can also use preprinted order sheets that allow staff to check appropriate boxes that describe the desired order. These forms lessen the time needed to write an order, eliminate misinterpretation of handwriting, and avoid spelling errors and confusion.

- Voice mail orders are not acceptable. When an order is not received directly, the nurse or pharmacist must call the prescriber back to get the order directly and read back the information.

- Organizations considering the use of technology as a means to comply with this goal must ensure that the system is capable of complying with all the steps of the read-back process (hear the order, write down the order, read back the order, receive confirmation that the order was received correctly) in a time frame that is consistent with safe, effective patient care.

Requirement 2B: Standardize a list of abbreviations, acronyms, and symbols that are not to be used throughout the organization. (Applicable to ambulatory care, assisted living, behavioral health care, critical access hospitals, disease-specific care, home care, hospitals, laboratories, long term care, office-based surgery)

Joint Commission Requirements

Organizations are only required to enforce the official "do not use" list of abbreviations, acronyms, and symbols that the Joint Commission introduced in January 1, 2004, and has reaffirmed as a minimum requirement for 2006 (see the list at http://www.jointcommission.org/PatientSafety/DoNotUseList). However, an organization may add other items to this minimum list to develop, with the involvement of physicians, an organization-specific list of unacceptable abbreviations, acronyms, and symbols not to use. (If an organization-specific list is created and used, surveyors

will evaluate whether the staff prohibits the additional abbreviations, acronyms, and symbols on their list.)

Since December 2004, the Joint Commission has made the following modifications to this requirement:

- The scope of the requirement has been reduced to apply only to orders (all orders, not just medication orders) and all medication-related documentation that is handwritten, uses free-text entry, or employs preprinted forms.

- The expected compliance for preprinted forms is 100%.

- The minimum expected level of compliance for handwritten and free-text entry orders and medication-related documentation is 90%.

- Organizations are no longer required to choose and enforce an additional three do-not-use abbreviations.

In addition, the Joint Commission has provided specific guidance to surveyors for scoring compliance, wherein surveyors will count occurrences of do-not-use abbreviations, acronyms, and symbols. The surveyors will follow the three occurrence rule, which entails the following:

- One occurrence equals one or more "slips" per clinician, per record. (One or more "slips" by the same clinician in the same record counts as a single occurrence.)

- Clarification of an order before implementation does not eliminate that occurrence from being counted.

- Immediate correction of the order by the clinician (before it is transcribed/transmitted) is not counted as an occurrence. However, correction after the order has been transcribed/transmitted results in that use of a prohibited abbreviation being counted as an occurrence.

- Three occurrences generate a requirement for improvement.

- Surveyors will score *satisfactory compliance* if only two occurrences or fewer are noted.

For 2006, the Joint Commission has relaxed the expectation that nurses and pharmacists must call the prescriber whenever a do-not-use abbreviation is used. However, the long-standing standards-based requirement remains that any unclear order must be clarified with the ordering practitioner. This is an explicit requirement of the Medication Management standards (MM.3.20, EP 5 and MM.4.10, EP 6) and is addressed more broadly for other types of orders in the Leadership standards (LD.3.60, EP 2). In the case of orders containing do-not-use abbreviations, the same requirements apply. That is, nurses and pharmacists exercise discretion to determine when an order is not clear and, in such cases, must contact the practitioner for clarification. Some prescribers might be unable or unwilling to stop using these prohibited terms. These are matters to be addressed and resolved by the medical staff. Leadership should work with its medical staff to eliminate the use of prohibited abbreviations. Nurses' and pharmacists' responses to the use of prohibited abbreviations should be guided by patient safety considerations, not by an assigned responsibility for monitoring and modifying prescriber behavior. It is not the responsibility of nurses or pharmacists to manage the behavior of prescribers. Joint Commission standards assign to the medical staff the responsibility for overseeing the quality and safety of patient care, treatment, and services provided by practitioners privileged through the medical staff process and, in particular, providing leadership in activities related to patient safety and improving performance associated with significant departures from established patterns of clinical practice.

This change in expectations for clarification of orders containing "do not use" abbreviations does not affect the scoring of Goal 2B. The scoring of this requirement has been and will continue to be based only on the actual use of the prohibited terms. Failure to contact the prescriber when there are concerns, issues, or questions about an order will be scored at MM.4.10, EP 6, (for medication orders) or at LD.3.60, EP 2 (for other types of orders). Failure of the medical staff to exercise its responsibilities for oversight of the actions of practitioners privileged through the medical staff process is scored at standards MS.2.10 and MS.3.10.

Compliance Solutions

Because this goal has existed since 2003, most organization leaders have effectively communicated the list of do-not-use abbreviations, acronyms, and symbols to the staff (see tips for educating and communicating to staff members about dangerous abbreviations, acronyms, and symbols at http://www.jointcommission.org/PatientSafety/NationalPatientSafetyGoals/abbr_tips.htm). However, it has proven difficult to change these behaviors in the staff. Even though they know which abbreviations, acronyms, and symbols not to use, many staff members are still continuing to "slip."

At this point, leaders should continue to enforce the do-not-use list by consistently monitoring staff compliance with this goal. Leaders can consider the following tips for enforcing and monitoring do-not-use abbreviations, acronyms, and symbols within their organizations:

- Review open records for evidence of eliminated use of prohibited abbreviations, symbols, and acronyms.

- Review closed records as necessary for validation of findings and track record assessment.

- Copy the page of the order or medical-related document with one or more do-not-use abbreviations and send it to the clinician who is not in compliance with the goal. Direct notification will help change individual compliance faster than tracking overall compliance rates. If the clinician continues to use unapproved abbreviations, acronyms, or symbols, the noncompliance should be documented in his or her credentials file.

Requirement 2C: Measure, assess, and, if appropriate, take action to improve the timeliness of reporting, and the timeliness of receipt by the responsible licensed caregiver, of critical test results and values. (Applicable to ambulatory care, behavioral health care, critical access hospitals, disease-specific care, home care, hospitals, laboratories, office-based surgery)

Joint Commission Requirements

The Joint Commission requires that critical tests and critical results be reported and

allocate sufficient time to this important task. Implement repeat-back or check-back techniques to make sure there is a common understanding about expectations. Encourage interactive questioning to allow for better information absorption. Keep the report patient-centered and avoid irrelevant details.

- **Standardize shift-to-shift and unit-to-unit reporting.** A consistent format increases the amount of information staff accurately record and recall and improves their ability to plan patient care. Organize the data with a sign-out checklist, script, or "at a glance" status display. Provide cues of important information to pass on that is otherwise likely to be forgotten in the chaos of shift or unit changes. Keep the report concise and accurate. Information included in hand-off communications varies by setting and discipline but can include a summary of the patient's current medical status, resuscitation status, recent lab values, allergies, a problem list, and a "to do" list for the covering physician or nurse. Get input from front-line staff to identify what should be included in the report.

- **Smooth hand-offs between settings.** The transition between settings of care (such as from the hospital to home, community, or long term care) can be undependable. To prevent problems, communicate with the physician when a patient is admitted and update him or her whenever the patient's status changes significantly. On discharge, provide the patient with information about discharge medications, discharge diagnoses, and results of procedures and labs. A simple follow-up call to the patient by a doctor, nurse, or pharmacist can prevent many postdischarge errors.

- **Use technology.** Communication systems that transmit information across settings and care providers bring consistency and coordination to care practices. For example, automated medication reconciliation between settings of care, such as physician office practices and the hospital, streamlines and increases safety during admissions and discharges.

Electronic medical records can facilitate transitions by providing consistent, accessi-

ble information about patients and their care. Staff should be able to readily access essential components of care, such as whether a newly ordered medication was administered, whether labs were done, or if a do-not-resuscitate order is in place.

Goal 3: Improve the Safety of Using Medications.

Requirement 3A: This goal has been retired for 2006 because of consistently high levels of compliance. However, this requirement continues as an element of performance under standard MM.2.20 in the "Medication Management" chapter in the accreditation manuals.

Requirement 3B: Standardize and limit the number of drug concentrations available in* the organization. (Applicable to ambulatory care, behavioral health care, critical access hospitals, disease-specific care, home care, hospitals, long term care, office-based surgery)

Joint Commission Requirements
An organization needs to limit the number of drug concentrations available in the organization and standardize those concentrations that are made available. Each organization will choose which drugs and which concentrations to make available based on its clinical need. With the exception of a few oral products that may be compounded by the pharmacy, all oral medications need to be limited to concentrations or dosages provided by the manufacturer. Thus, this goal primarily relates to injectable solutions of drugs administered by infusion.

Compliance Solutions
When multiple concentrations of a drug are clinically necessary (such as on a pediatric unit), staff should take special precautions to avoid dosing errors. For example, the order should specify actual drug dose, not volume, and the dose calculation—including specific data elements, such as the patient's weight, dose per unit weight, and rate of administration—should be written as part of the order. This provides sufficient information for the pharmacist who reviews the order and

---

* Insert "used by" in place of "available in" for **home care**.

prepares the medication and the nurse who administers the medication to recalculate the dose as a check.

Pediatric and neonatal units should not use the "Rule of Six" to calculate patient-specific drug concentrations. To achieve a given dose of an infused drug while being compliant with Goal 3B, organizations must vary the rate of infusion and keep the concentration constant (standardized). The Rule of Six varies the concentration of the drug while keeping the rate constant, which is not in compliance with Goal 3B.

Although many organization requests for continued use of the Rule of Six have been approved on a temporary basis, organizations must be committed to creating and implementing a plan to change over to standardized drug concentrations. Because potential risks associated with revising an established process always exist, the Joint Commission conferred with experts in the pediatric and neonatal critical care fields—including the American Academy of Pediatrics, the National Association of Children's Hospitals and Related Institutions, and the American Society of Health-System Pharmacists—and has set a three-year transition period for the move to standardized concentrations. All providers are expected to have completed the transition by **December 31, 2008**.

Requirement 3C: Identify and, at a minimum, annually review a list of look-alike/sound-alike drugs used in* the organization, and take action to prevent errors involving the interchange of these drugs. (Applicable to ambulatory care, behavioral health care, critical access hospitals, home care, hospitals, long term care, office-based surgery)

Joint Commission Requirements

The Joint Commission has developed a list of look-alike, sound-alike medications that create the greatest risk for medication error (http://www.jointcommission.org). Organizations must choose 10 pairs of look-alike, sound-alike medications from this list that are relevant to the organization's services and take action to prevent errors involving the interchange of these drugs. An organization may choose

to include more look-alike, sound-alike medications on its organization-specific list, but those medications must be in addition to the 10 pairs chosen from the Joint Commission's list.

If an organization has reason to believe that other drug pairs present a higher risk to its patients (based on the services provided), or is unable to identify 10 pairs of look-alike/sound-alike drugs that are relevant to the organization's services, then it must present this for consideration by the Joint Commission. To do so, the organization must submit a Request for Review of an Alternative Approach by filling out the form located at http://www.jointcommission.org/PatientSafety/NationalPatientSafetyGoals/06_npsg_rfr.htm.

Compliance Solutions

To ensure that the correct medication is being administered, be sure that staff members are well informed, especially because so many drug names sound alike. To reduce look-alike/sound-alike drug misunderstandings, the staff should consider the following:

■ Provide both the brand and generic drug names on the medication label and patient's chart.

■ Consider the potential for dispensing errors when adding medications to the organization's formulary.

■ Group drugs by category rather than by alphabetical order.

■ Add alerts to the pharmacy computer system.

■ Look into carousel technology for pharmacy inventory and storage. With this technology, when a pharmacist is fulfilling a medication order, the carousel spins to the correct storage area and a light directs the pharmacist to the exact bin where the medication is stored.

■ Use brightly colored labels, TALL-MAN lettering, and physical separation to differentiate drugs during dispensing activities.

■ Include in the order the indication for the medication to help the pharmacist identify potential errors. Explain to the

* Replace "in" with "by" for **home care**.

patient the purpose of the medication he or she will be taking and, if possible, describe what the pill will look like.

NEW! Requirement 3D: Label all medications, medication containers (for example, syringes, medicine cups, basins), or other solutions on and off the sterile field in perioperative and other procedural settings. (Applicable to ambulatory care, critical access hospitals, hospitals, and office-based surgery)

Joint Commission Requirements

Errors have resulted from medications and other solutions removed from their original containers and placed into unlabeled containers. Medications or other solutions in unlabeled containers cannot be identified. This unsafe practice neglects basic principles of medication management safety yet has been routine with respect to medications transferred to the *sterile field* or used during the administration of anesthesia in many organizations. Therefore, when medications or solutions are transferred from the original packaging to another container, the new container must be labeled. An exception to this would be when a solution or medication is poured or drawn up from a properly labeled container into another container or syringe and is used (administered) immediately—in these situations, labeling is not required. Medications and solutions used in any procedural setting, whether on or off the *sterile field*, must be labeled even if only one medication or solution is being used.

All original containers from medications or solutions must remain available for reference in the perioperative area until the procedure is completed. After the procedure is complete, the contents held in all labeled containers on the sterile field must be discarded. In addition, medications and solutions both on and off the *sterile field* (and their labels) must be reviewed by personnel who are going on breaks or at shift change.

Labels include drug name, strength, amount (if not apparent from the container), expiration date when not used within 24 hours, and expiration time when expiration occurs in less than 24 hours. **Note:** *Expiration date and time are rarely necessary in procedural settings.*

All labels are verified both verbally and visually by two qualified individuals

Goal 3: Specifically for Your Program...

Home care: Goal 3B applies to medications stored in the home care organization, not to medications already dispensed by a pharmacy to the patient's residence. In addition, organizations should focus on preparations of insulin, heparin, antibiotics, and antineoplastics.

Ambulatory care: For Goal 3B, organizations should focus on preparations of insulin, heparin, antibiotics, and antineoplastics.

Long term care: Goal 3B applies to all medications stored in the organization, even medications dispensed to the organization by an outside pharmacy. Residents are often at risk for Goal 3C because they are taking so many medications. The staff should separate medications for each resident to also prevent the possibility of a look-alike, sound-alike resident.

when the person preparing the medication is not the person administering the medication.

Compliance Solutions

Medications and solutions that fall under Goal 3D include but are not limited to the following:

- Prescription medications and any other product designated by the Food and Drug Administration (FDA) as a drug

- Diagnostic and contrast agents used on or administered to persons to diagnose, treat, or prevent disease or other abnormal conditions

- Radioactive medications

- Respiratory therapy treatments

- Parenteral nutrition

- Blood derivatives

- IV solutions (plain or with electrolytes and/or drugs)

- Chemicals and reagents such as formalin, saline, sterile water, Lugol's solution, radiopaque dyes, glutaraldehyde, and chlorhexidine

In addition, organizations can adhere to the following tips for creating, using, and enforcing the use of labels on medications and solutions:

- Include on the label the name and strength of the medication or solution

- Develop distinct labels or purchase commercially available sterile labels.

- Have two qualified individuals verify labels both verbally and visually.

- Label medications/solutions at the time they are prepared.

- Do not label more than one medication or solution at the same time.

- Discard any medications or solutions that are found without labels.

- Have no distraction during medication preparation.

Goal 4: Eliminate Wrong-site, Wrong-patient, and Wrong-procedure Surgery. (Applicable to disease-specific care)

Goal 5: Improve the Safety of Using Infusion Pumps.

Requirement 5A: Ensure free-flow protection on all general-use and patient-controlled analgesia (PCA) intravenous infusion pumps used in the organization.

This requirement has been retired because of consistently high levels of compliance and because problems with availability of free-flow–protected administration sets for certain types of pumps have been resolved by the manufacturers.

Goal 6: Improve the effectiveness of clinical alarm systems. (Applicable to disease-specific care)

Goal 7: Reduce the Risk of Health Care–Associated Infections.

Requirement 7A: Comply with current Centers for Disease Control and Prevention

(CDC) hand hygiene guidelines.[*][†] (Applicable to ambulatory care, assisted living, behavioral health care, critical access hospitals, disease-specific care, home care, hospitals, laboratories, long term care, office-based surgery)

Joint Commission Requirements

Organizations must comply with all current "Category I" recommendations (including IA, IB, and IC) in the CDC hand hygiene guidelines. (Find the CDC's full report at http://www.cdc.gov/handhygiene). The report is extremely detailed and well documented. The specific recommendations referred to in the health care–associated infections goal are on pages 31 through 34 of the report. In general, the CDC hand hygiene guidelines require staff to decontaminate hands with a hygienic hand rub or by washing with disinfectant soap before and after direct contact with a patient or objects immediately around a patient.

Compliance with the hand hygiene guidelines will be surveyed through interviews with caregiver staff and direct observation. A minimum of 90% compliance will be expected. The surveyors will follow the three occurrence rule, which entails the following:

- One occurrence equals one observation of noncompliance with CDC Category I recommendations.

- Three occurrences equal a requirement for improvement.

- Surveyors will score *satisfactory compliance* if only two occurrences or fewer are noted.

Compliance Solutions

Because hand hygiene is the most effective way to reduce infection transmission, organizations can use the following tips to help improve infection control:

- Encourage patients and families to speak up and ask health care workers to clean their hands

---

[*] Organizations are required to comply with all category IA, IB, and IC CDC hand hygiene recommendations.

[†] Add "when providing services to a high-risk population or administering physical care" for **behavioral health care**.

- Place posters by sinks and in bathrooms to remind staff to wash their hands. Also, provide role models to motivate staff to comply with hand hygiene practices.

- Monitor hand hygiene adherence and provide feedback to personnel about staff performance or monitor the volume of alcohol-based hand rub used per 1,000 patient days

- Make improved adherence to hand hygiene practices an institutional priority and provide appropriate administrative support and financial resources

- Implement a multidisciplinary program designed to improve adherence to recommended hand hygiene practices

- Residents in long term care settings can be a source of infection. Encourage resident handwashing after toileting, before eating, and so forth, to reduce the likelihood of cross-contamination.

Several studies have confirmed the efficacy of alcohol-based hand rub (ABHR) and have demonstrated higher levels of compliance with hand hygiene recommendations when ABHR dispensers are located just outside of the entrances to patients' rooms. In most organizations, this would result in placement of dispensers in egress corridors. The Centers for Medicare & Medicaid Services (CMS) and the National Fire Protection Association (NFPA) have recently determined that it is allowable for organizations to place ABHR *gel* dispensers outside patients' rooms in egress corridors.

The Joint Commission's official stand on the use of ABHR is described below.

ABHR *Gel:* Dispensers in Egress Corridors

The Joint Commission allows the installation of ABHR gel dispensers in corridors provided that the following conditions are met:

- The corridor width is 6 feet or greater and dispensers are at least 4 feet apart.

- The dispensers are not installed over or directly adjacent to an ignition source such as an electrical outlet or switch. *Adjacent* is defined as being at least

> **Goal 7: Specifically for Your Program...**
>
> *Behavioral health care:* For Goal 7A, organizations should teach their clients about hand hygiene as well. In addition, a death or major permanent loss of function associated with a health care–associated infection usually only occurs in inpatient programs such as crisis stabilization, residential, corrections, forensics, and opioid treatment programs. Although sentinel events may be infrequent in outpatient settings, Goal 7B is still applicable.

6 inches from the center of the dispenser to an ignition source.

- In locations with carpeted floor coverings, dispensers installed directly over carpeted surfaces are permitted only in sprinklered smoke compartments.

ABHR *Gel:* Permissible Volume

Permissible volumes of an ABHR *gel* are as follows:

- Each smoke compartment may contain a maximum aggregate of 10 gallons (37.8 liters) of ABHR gel in dispensers and a maximum of 5 gallons (18.9 liters) in storage.

- The maximum individual dispenser fluid capacity is 0.3 gallons (1.2 liters) for dispensers in rooms, corridors, and areas open to corridors.

- The maximum dispenser size for individual dispensers in areas designated as suites of rooms is 0.5 gallons (2.0 liters).

ABHR *Foam:* Permissible Location and Volume

Industry experts have indicated that small-quantity ABHR *foam* dispensers *may* be equivalent to the ABHR *gel.* Therefore, pending further review, the Joint Commission will allow use of any ABHR *foam* installation that meets the location criteria stated above for ABHR *gel.* Volumes of ABHR *foam* are based on suppliers' recommendations and in no case exceed the permissible volumes for ABHR *gel* as defined above. In the event that subsequent testing demonstrates a safety concern relating to the installation of *foam* dispensers in egress corridors, the Joint Commission reserves the right to modify its position on the acceptability of such installations. In that event, previously installed dispensers would be subject to the newer restrictions; that is, they would not be

---

Sidebar 2-1. Strategies for Managing as Sentinel Events All Identified Cases of Unanticipated Death or Major Permanent Loss of Function Associated with a Health Care–Associated Infection

1. Review your sentinel event policy. Revisit the organization policy covering management of sentinel events and amend it, if necessary, to explicitly include cases in which a health care-associated infection resulted in an unanticipated death or major permanent loss of function. A simple statement, like the following, emphasizes the importance of patient harm:

A sentinel event will result if a patient who has a low mortality risk experiences a health care–associated infection that contributes to an unanticipated death or major permanent loss of function.

Inform infection control practitioners, physicians, and other front-line staff of the organization's commitment to reducing harm to patients from infection-related sentinel events.

2. Continue ongoing infection surveillance. The Joint Commission does not expect or require any increase in surveillance activities. An organization's current surveillance should include a review of all deaths and events that may be linked to a health care-associated infection, such as a surgical infection or bloodstream infection. Major or permanent loss of function will be rare, but can be seen with endocarditis, *Aspergillus fumigatus*, or neurosurgical conditions, among others.

3. Identify infection-related sentinel events. Determining whether a patient's death or injury was unanticipated is generally based on the patient's condition at the time of admission to the organization. A death or major permanent loss of function is considered a sentinel event if the outcome was not the result of the natural course of the patient's illness or underlying condition(s) that existed at the time of admission.

Establish screening criteria as to whether an infection is "causative" or "contributory" (per International Classification of Diseases (ICD), Tenth Revision definitions). For example, an otherwise healthy patient who is admitted for an elective procedure but who develops a wound infection, becomes septic, and dies should be considered a sentinel event. However, cases in which the patient is immunocompromised or elderly with multiple comorbidities are more difficult to classify.

If surveillance produces a case in which a health care-associated infection was indeed a causal factor in a patient's death or loss of function, the organization must manage it as a sentinel event.

4. Conduct a credible RCA. The RCA is not just an analysis of the infection, but of the event itself. Examine why the patient acquired the infection and why the patient died or suffered major permanent loss of function. Use the analysis to identify system and process factors that through appropriate redesign can reduce the risk of serious adverse patient outcomes even as the risk of a health care-associated infection remains high.

Although the infection control professional's participation could be very beneficial, the team conducting the analysis should be multidisciplinary and include front-line staff most involved in the process. The RCA will help identify contributing factors, root cause(s), and effective control measures to reduce the risk of recurrence.

5. Implement any needed actions to reduce future risk. One product of a credible and successful RCA will be action plans to prevent recurrence. A thorough review of the literature will help the team base action plans on best practices and appropriate standards. Implement improvements to reduce risk in all areas where applicable, not just where the event occurred.

"grandfathered" and noncompliant installations would have to be removed.

The Joint Commission's official stance on ABHR is based on the latest information in the NFPA 101-2000, *Life Safety Code® (LSC)*.* As with other areas of the *LSC*, organizations may not meet all the requirements completely but may still provide an equivalent level of safety through assessing and managing the specific construction, systems, or operation of an area. Likewise, an organization that cannot meet all the requirements outlined here may perform a product-specific risk assessment of the ABHR product using product literature and determine alternative methods to achieve an equivalent level of safety.

Please refer to *Perspectives* for updates on this issue.

---

* *Life Safety Code®* is a registered trademark of the National Fire Protection Association, Quincy, Massachusetts.

Regardless of which measures organizations take to meet this goal, they should measure and monitor compliance through observing staff, interviewing staff and patients, and monitoring the volume of alcohol-based hand rub used per 1,000 patient days.

Requirement 7B: Manage as sentinel events all identified cases of unanticipated death or major permanent loss of function associated with a health care–associated infection. (Applicable to ambulatory care, assisted living, behavioral health care, critical access hospitals, disease-specific care, home care, hospitals, laboratories, long term care, office-based surgery)

Joint Commission Requirements

Requirement 7B is not a new requirement but a reminder that any unanticipated death or major permanent loss of function is a sentinel event *even if* it is associated with a health care–associated infection (HAI). Thus, a root cause analysis (RCA) should be conducted for each of these events to determine strategies that may reduce future risk.

Although the requirement for an RCA is also not new, many cases that meet this definition have not been considered sentinel events—apparently because infection was associated with the outcome. In other words, some in health care have assumed that the presence of infection excludes a case from consideration as a sentinel event. This exclusion is not, nor has it ever been, an intended exclusion. As a result, there are very few cases of infection-associated sentinel events in the Joint Commission's Sentinel Event Database (in relation to other types of sentinel events and to the number of infection-associated cases reported to be occurring annually). The Joint Commission believes that managing these cases as sentinel events will provide additional information, not so much about the infection itself but about managing patients at risk for infection and who have acquired an infection. In this manner, this goal will contribute to reducing the risk of patient harm from HAIs. (See Sidebar 2-1 on page 45 for strategies to manage these instances as sentinel events.)

Compliance Solutions

Determining whether a death is related to an HAI can be difficult, but in fact, establishing that relationship is not necessary for determining whether a death is a sentinel event. A death or major permanent loss of function should be considered a sentinel event if the outcome was not the result of the natural course of illness or underlying condition at the time of admission. If at the time of admission, the patient's condition is such that he or she has a high likelihood of not surviving the episode of care, then that patient's death would not be considered a sentinel event. The following suggestions and clarifications will help organizations build compliance with this requirement:

- Organizations should review all in-hospital deaths to identify those that were unanticipated. If an HAI was part of the clinical picture, an infection control professional should participate in the RCA.

- Organizations do not have to change their surveillance methods to be compliant with Goal 7B.

- Managing these cases as sentinel events is complementary to, not a replacement for, the traditional rate-based analysis of HAIs.

- An RCA is only required for HAIs that result in death or major injury.

- When conducting the RCAs for sentinel events associated with HAIs, the organization should remember that the objective is a comprehensive analysis of the care of the patient, not just the infection itself.

- The determination of whether an adverse outcome was "unanticipated" is based on the condition of the patient at the time of entry into the organization.

Goal 8: Accurately and Completely Reconcile Medications Across the Continuum of Care.

Requirement 8A: Implement a process for obtaining and documenting a complete list of the patient's current medications upon the patient's admission* to the organization and with the involvement of the patient. This process includes a comparison of the medications the organization provides to those on the list.† (Applicable to ambulatory care, assisted living, behavioral health care, critical access hospitals, disease-specific care, home care, hospitals, long term care, office-based surgery)

Requirement 8B: A complete list of the patient's medication is communicated to the next provider of service when a patient is referred or transferred to another setting, service, practitioner, or level of care within or outside the organization. (Applicable to ambulatory care, assisted living, behavioral health care, critical access hospitals, disease-specific care, home care, hospitals, long term care, office-based surgery)

Joint Commission Requirements

Reconciling medications requires the following four steps:

---

* Insert "entry" in place of "admission" for **ambulatory care, behavioral health care,** and **office-based surgery.**

† For **home care,** replace the previous sentence with "This process includes a comparison of the medications ordered for the patient while under the care of the organization to those on the list."

1. Develop a complete and accurate list of the patient's medications (maintain this exact list separately throughout the rest of the steps).

2. Compare (or reconcile) the listed medications (created in step 1) with any new orders for medications. Check for the following potential errors: omission of a medication, duplication of medications, possible drug interaction, and name/dose/route confusion.

3. Create a new list of medications that now includes the patient's current medications. Continue to update this list as orders change throughout the patient's length of stay.

4. Upon discharge or transfer to another organization, use the original list (step 1) and the updated list (step 3) to reconcile with the discharge medications and provide a complete and accurate list of all the medications the patient is to be on following discharge to the next provider of care as well as to the patient.

When staff members are compiling information about a patient's current medications, they must, to the extent possible, involve the patient in this process. In addition, staff members are expected to communicate the updated medication reconciliation information to the next provider of service. The updated medication list that will be transferred to the next provider of care should contain only the medications to be continued following discharge or transfer—not the medications that were taken only while in the organization. Surveyors will make sure that this standardized process for compiling, reviewing, and communicating a patient's complete list of medications has been fully implemented.

To completely reconcile medications, staff members must compare what the patient is taking at the time of admission or entry with what the organization is planning to prescribe. Ideally, organizations will not prescribe a medication before attaining the complete list of medications that the patient is currently taking. However, if there is an urgent situation in which the resulting delay would harm the patient, an organization can prescribe without attaining the complete list of current medications. After staff members

stabilize the patient, they should take steps to compile a complete list of the patient's medications and compare it to the medications currently being provided. This process will help avoid errors of transcription, omission, duplication of therapy, and drug–drug and drug–disease interactions.

An important aspect of the reconciliation process at the time of discharge or transfer from the organization is comparison of the medications to be continued postdischarge/posttransfer with the list of medications the patient was taking before entry into the organization. This will help to avoid duplication and ensure that necessary ongoing therapy is not discontinued.

The only required documentation is the compiled list of medications. However, organizations will likely establish their own additional documentation requirements to implement and manage the reconciliation process.

Compliance Solutions

Medication reconciliation is important because medications have become more numerous and complicated, there are more physicians prescribing different medications to the same patient, and patients are no longer going to a single local pharmacy to fill their prescriptions. In addition, reconciling medications actually reduces the duplication of work because one person gathers the information and passes that information along to other caregivers rather than each caregiver gathering the same information.

Many organizations have developed helpful solutions to meet this goal and its requirements, including the following:

■ Create a medication reconciliation form, to be used as a template for gathering information about current medications. (The Massachusetts Coalition for the Prevention of Medical Errors provides examples of forms along with instructions for designing a form at http://www.macoalition.org/Initiatives/RMToolkit.shtml). The form should let staff members visually see that the medications have been reconciled.

■ Include the reasons for changing medications in the reconciliation information so that the next provider of care understands why the patient was transferred to a new type of medication.

■ When interviewing a patient about medications taken, remember to ask about over-the-counter drugs, herbals, and dietary supplements. Patients may not consider these "medications," but they are. Other commonly missed medications are eye drops, inhalers, patches, and contraceptives.

■ Involve the pharmacist in compiling the patient's medication list when the patient is taking more than a certain number of medications (for example, more than 10 medications).

■ Put ordering prescribers in charge of the process—that is, they will not order medications until they receive the patient's current list of medications—but have nurses and pharmacists contribute significantly to the process.

■ Include medication reconciliation information in the change-of-shift procedures as well as in the physician's progress notes.

■ Improve the interviewing process with patients to find out what medications they are taking. Prompt patients with open-ended, specific questions about their health as well as their medications. For example, go down the list of a patient's conditions, asking what medications he or she takes for each, or prompt the patient for medications prescribed by each of his or her physicians.

■ Educate the community (possibly through primary care physicians) so that patients know to bring their medication list as well as their insurance cards when entering a health care organization.

■ Establish time frames for reconciling different types of medications so that

caregivers are not called early in the morning to reconcile a medication that could have waited until business hours. For example, medications can be classified as needing reconciliation within 4 hours, within 24 hours, or before the next prescribed dose.

■ For outpatient services, staff members do not need to document a medication list or reconcile medications when a patient's medications are not relevant to the services provided. However, if medications are prescribed or the risk or results of the procedure might be affected by medications, then the medication list should be obtained from the patient.

■ When collecting data on whether medications are being reconciled, use open charts (charts of patients that have been on the unit for 24 hours) to prevent errors immediately.

■ Before automating a medication reconciliation process, organization leaders must make sure a stable paper process exists. Leaders should also consider a careful design that designates who can enter the information initially and who can update and change information so that new errors are not introduced.

■ Keep the staff focused on reconciliation by producing a monthly report that honors staff members who caught potentially dangerous medication problems by reconciling.

In addition, organizations can find helpful resources at the Web sites of the Massachusetts Coalition (http://www.macoalition.org) and the Institute for Healthcare Improvement (http://www.ihi.org).

Goal 9: Reduce the Risk of Patient Harm Resulting from Falls.

On the advice of the Sentinel Event Advisory Group, Goal 9A *(Assess and periodically reassess each patient's risk for falling, including the potential risk associated with the patient's medication regimen, and take action to address any identified risks)* has been retired and assisted living, critical access

Goal 9: Specifically for Your Program...

Home care and long term care: It is especially important to identify medications the patient might be taking for which there would be side effects such as drowsiness, motor disturbances, and ataxia that would make patients prone to falls.

Critical access hospitals and hospitals: Reassess patients in the postoperative setting for change in risk for falls after surgery (sedation places patients at risk for falls). In addition, hospitals should consider the pediatric population in their fall reduction programs.

Long Term Care: Consider bed adaptations and a safe space layout with low beds and mattresses or pads placed on the floor.

hospitals, disease-specific care, home care, hospitals, and long term care organizations are now required to implement only Goal 9B *(Implement a fall reduction program and evaluate the effectiveness of the program)*. This change in requirements gives organizations more flexibility to comply with the overall goal of reducing the risk of patient harm resulting from falls.

Requirement 9B: Implement a fall reduction program and evaluate the effectiveness of the program. (Applicable to assisted living, critical access hospitals, disease-specific care, home care, hospitals, long term care)

Joint Commission Requirements

For appropriate settings of care and patient populations, the fall reduction program will still include the assessment and reassessment of a patient's risk for falls. However, Goal 9B should give organizations more flexibility to comply with the overall goal of reducing the risk of patient harm resulting from falls. In this way, organizations must implement a fall reduction program and evaluate the effectiveness of the program. As appropriate, this program should include an assessment process, risk reduction strategies, transfer protocols, in-services, involvement of patients/families in education, and evaluation of environment of care issues.

Compliance Solutions

Organizations that have been implementing fall reduction programs have found the following tips helpful:

- Identify some of the drugs/drug classes that are most frequently associated with an increased risk for falling. Some suggested medication classifications are hypnotics, sedatives, analgesics, psychotropics, antihypertensives, laxatives, and diuretics.

- Use a transfer protocol to guide the staff in how a patient or resident can be transferred safely from a wheelchair, cart, stretcher, or bed.

- Evaluate how long it takes for the staff to address patient calls (and shorten that time, if necessary) and ensure that food, liquid, and toileting needs are met.

- Promote a normal sleep pattern for patients.

- Use a reliable and valid instrument to predict and identify prone-to-fall patients.

- Communicate a patient's fall risk to the patient and family and remind patients to call for assistance before getting out of bed or getting up from a chair (reassure them that this does not bother staff).

- Understand the patient by knowing that some are prone to falls because of recent changes in levels of independence, slow adaptation to environmental changes, short-term memory changes, poor impulse control, sensory changes (for example, visual, auditory, balance, awareness of elimination needs), fine motor changes, and communication difficulties.

- Make sure there is enough staff coverage during shift changes.

- Consider the environment of care by making sure the patient's needed objects are accessible at all times, improving lighting, controlling noise, moving higher-risk patients closer to the nurses' station, avoiding slippery floors or loose carpeting, and installing handrails.

- Provide visual cueing (for example, special colored ID bands, identifier on the door or bed) for staff members so that they know which patients are at high risk for falls.

Goal 10: Reduce the Risk of Influenza and Pneumococcal Disease in Older Adults.

Requirement 10A: Develop and implement a protocol for administration and documentation of the flu vaccine. (Applicable to assisted living, disease-specific care, long term care)

Requirement 10B: Develop and implement a protocol for administration and documentation of the pneumococcus vaccine. (Applicable to assisted living, disease-specific care, long term care)

Requirement 10C: Develop and implement a protocol to identify new cases of influenza and to manage an outbreak. (Applicable to assisted living, disease-specific care, long term care)

Joint Commission Requirements

This goal requires that long term care and assisted living organizations adhere to the following steps:

1. Develop appropriate protocols for determining whether to vaccinate a person for influenza (usually on a yearly basis) or pneumonia (usually a one-time-only immunization).

2. Develop and implement a protocol to identify new cases of influenza and to manage an outbreak

Compliance Solutions

Although influenza vaccine shortages can be frustrating, the special populations that are featured in this goal usually take a high-priority for receiving vaccinations, making this goal achievable despite vaccine shortages.

When evaluating interventions that may effectively reduce the risk of influenza and pneumococcal disease in older adults, one of the first steps is to consider preventive measures. If your health care organization has ambulatory services such as primary care clinics, consider developing performance measures to remind health care providers to offer both flu and pneumococcus vaccines to older adult patients. Have

staff and physicians review the medical record in advance or during the patient's visit to ensure that the patient had been offered the vaccinations. If the patient refuses the vaccinations, document that the benefits of the vaccine were discussed and that the patient refused administration of the vaccinations. If the patient has received the vaccinations, include that information as part of the admission process. If the patient does not remember whether he or she received a vaccination, the organization should administer the vaccine again. (The CDC has found little data to support any significant increase in complications for patients who have been reimmunized).

Organizations can review the number of cases of older adults who contracted influenza and pneumococcal disease during their stay to identify where they were vaccinated. Results can be trended for significant patterns such as vaccinations from the clinic, the providers, and so forth. Feedback can then be provided to the ambulatory sites. For organizations that do not own their clinics, it is just as important for patients to be assessed for these immunizations on admission. These data can be shared with providers at the appropriate medical staff meetings. In addition, organizations need to define the age range of "older adult" to ensure consistency of data collection and data analysis.

Organizations should consider offering vaccinations for older adults who come through urgent care facilities and emergency departments because of other health care issues. With the number of uninsured patients increasing, and as more older adults use urgent care and emergency departments as a source of primary care, these avenues may be the only way for some adults to receive the immunizations.

Organizations should continuously monitor the success of their efforts to prevent these diseases by capturing and analyzing data. The performance measures should be reported to those who regularly oversee infection control and to the organizations' performance improvement infrastructure. The data should also be shared with staff, as appropriate, so they can see the success rate of reducing the risk of influenza and pneumococcal disease in older patients.

Goal 11: Reduce the Risk of Surgical Fires.

Requirement 11A: Educate staff, including operating licensed independent practitioners and anesthesia providers, on how to control heat sources and manage fuels, and establish guidelines to minimize oxygen concentration under drapes. (Applicable to ambulatory care, office-based surgery)

Joint Commission Requirements

Three elements are required for a fire to ignite—fuel, oxygen, and heat. Staff education is key to proper management of these elements, and proper education can help to significantly reduce the risk for surgical fires. It is important to educate staff, including operating licensed independent practitioners and anesthesia providers, on how to control heat sources and manage fuels. A wide range of combustibles and flammables are found in the surgical suite, and education on the use of alcohol or alcohol-based products can help reduce risk. Proper management of oxygen and surgical devices is also necessary to prevent fires. Organizations must establish guidelines to minimize oxygen concentration under drapes and to ensure that preparation solutions, which may be alcohol based, are dry before the patient is draped.

Surveyors will determine compliance with this requirement by doing the following:

- Interviewing perioperative staff members, surgeons, and anesthesia providers

- Observing the surgical environment

- Reviewing selected personnel and staff training files

Compliance Solutions

The following tips can help organizations prevent surgical fires:

- Inform staff members, including surgeons and anesthesiologists, about the importance of controlling heat sources by (1) following laser and electrosurgical unit safety practices, (2) managing fuels by allowing sufficient time for patient preparation, and (3) establishing guidelines for minimizing oxygen concentration under the drapes.

- Develop implementing and testing procedures to ensure appropriate response by all members of the surgical team to fires in the operating room.

- Use proper procedures to prepare patients. Any exposed body hair and skin should be covered with a water-soluble lubricant. The individual's eyes can be covered with swabs soaked in sodium chloride.

- Make sure equipment is maintained and used properly. All electrosurgical equipment should be calibrated and inspected frequently.

- Question the need for 100% oxygen during surgery, especially facial surgery.

- Do not drape the patient until all flammable preps are fully dry.

- Soak gauze or sponges used with tracheal tubes to resist ignition.

- Control heat sources by holstering surgical equipment or placing it in standby modes (For example, the surgeon might place the electrosurgical electrodes in a holster.)

- Take special precaution to prevent fires during anesthesia induction.

- Include fire emergency procedures in the presurgery checklist.

- Empower the surgical staff to have the confidence to warn the surgeon that there might be the possibility for a fire during the surgery.

- Reorganize the floor plan of the operating room, considering the location of fire extinguishers, alarm pull boxes, fire doors, oxygen shutoffs, and potential evacuation routes.

- Be aware that alcohol-based skin preps (ABSPs) are flammable.

Organizations are strongly encouraged to report any instances of surgical fires as a means of raising awareness and ultimately preventing the recurrence of fires. Reports can be made to the Joint Commission, ECRI (formerly the Emergency Care Research Institute), the Food and Drug Administration, and state agencies, among other organizations.

Goal 12: Implementation of Applicable National Patient Safety Goals and Associated Requirements by Components and Practitioner Sites.

Requirement 12A: Inform and encourage components and practitioner sites to implement the applicable National Patient Safety Goals and associated requirements. (Applicable to integrated delivery systems, managed care organizations, preferred provider organizations)*

Joint Commission Requirements

Integrated delivery systems, managed care organizations, and preferred provider organizations should assess all National Patient Safety Goals and requirements to see which are applicable to the components and practitioner sites that comprise their networks. Integrated delivery systems, managed care organizations, and preferred provider organizations should communicate information on the National Patient Safety Goals and requirements to their applicable components (ambulatory care, office-based surgery, behavioral health care, critical access hospitals, home care, hospitals, laboratories, long term care, and practitioner sites) and actively encourage compliance with applicable requirements by those components and practitioner sites.

Compliance Solutions

Organizations should be familiar with the National Patient Safety Goals and know which goals are applicable to their components or practitioner sites. In addition, organizations should inform their components and practitioner sites about the goals by doing any of the following:

* The Joint Commission has discontinued its assisted living, integrated delivery system, managed care organization, and preferred provider organization accreditation programs effective January 1, 2006. However, the Joint Commission will continue to provide a full array of support services and oversight to organizations accredited under these programs through the end of each organization's respective accreditation award period. No new accreditation surveys or resurveys under this program will be conducted.

- Incorporating the topic into provider handbooks or newsletters

- Administering contractual performance evaluations

- Conducting audits of components and practitioner sites

Finally, organizations should encourage component and practitioner sites to implement the goals.

New! Goal 13: Encourage the Active Involvement of Patients and Their Families in the Patient's Own Care as a Patient Safety Strategy.

NEW! Requirement 13A: Define and communicate the means for patients and their families to report concerns about safety and encourage them to do so. (Applicable to disease-specific care, laboratories, home care)

Joint Commission Requirements

Interactive communication with patients and families about all aspects of their care, treatment, and services is an important characteristic of a culture of safety. When patients are engaged as active participants in their own care, they are more aware of possible complications and treatment choices. Patients and their families can be an important source of feedback about actual or potential adverse events because, with their unique perspective, they often observe things that busy health care providers might not. By encouraging communication about errors or near misses, patients and their families can be effectively integrated into an organization's patient safety work processes.

Compliance Solutions

Just as organization cultures are changing to promote a safer environment, patients are also changing to become more active in their own care. When educated properly, many patients and families welcome the opportunity to contribute to efforts to prevent or recover from systems failure. For example, patients and families can play important roles in helping their health care providers (1) reach an accurate diagnosis, (2) ensure that treatment plans are appropriate and effective, and (3) identify side effects or adverse events quickly and take appropriate action. Organization reporting systems that do not provide pathways for patient reporting miss the opportunity to capture information that can contribute to error prevention and quality improvement work.

The following tips can help improve patient communication and education:

- Explain to patients and their families that the single most important way they can help health care providers to prevent errors is to be active members of the health care team.

- Provide explicit information to patients and their families about the risks associated with their particular procedures or courses of care and what to watch out for during or after particular procedures or courses of care.

- Provide written information about the side effects that a medicine could cause so that patients will be better prepared if known side effects do occur or if something unexpected happens instead. Encourage patients to report a problem right away so that they can get help before it gets worse.

- Explain to patients that they should not assume that no news is good news after they have a test. Patients can help by asking about the results and reporting to providers when they don't receive any results.

- Through interactive communication, encourage the patient and family to feel comfortable enough to speak up about any concerns they have about errors or their quality of care.

- Encourage patients and their families to learn about their conditions and treatments by asking their physicians and nurses and by using other reliable sources.

For more information on involving patients in their care, view the Joint Commission's

Speak Up™ initiatives at http://www.jointcommission.org/ PatientSafety/Speakup.

New! Goal 14: Prevent Health Care–Associated Pressure Ulcers (Decubitus Ulcers).

NEW! Requirement 14A: Assess and periodically reassess each patient's risk for developing a pressure ulcer (decubitus ulcer) and take action to address any identified risks. (Applicable to long term care)

Joint Commission Requirements

Pressure ulcers continue to be problematic in health care, and the incidence of pressure ulcer rates for long term care is 2.2% to 23.9%. Many pressure ulcers can be prevented, and deterioration at Stage I can be halted. The use of clinical practice guidelines can effectively identify patients at risk for pressure ulcers and define early intervention for prevention of ulcers.

Compliance Solutions

A systematic risk assessment tool, such as the Braden Scale or Norton Scale, can help improve assessment and identification of at-risk patients. An effective plan for preventing pressure ulcers includes the following:

- Recognizing at-risk individuals and the specific factors that place them at risk

- Identifying a prevention program that is specific to each at-risk individual

- Maintaining and improving tissue tolerance to pressure to prevent injury

- Protecting against the adverse effects of external mechanical forces

- Meeting the patient's nutritional support needs

- Reducing the incidence of pressure ulcers through education programs

Some organizations create pressure ulcer (or wound care) programs to place emphasis on the importance of preventing pressure ulcers and improve the consistency of care for patients with pressure ulcers.

Preventing pressure ulcers requires a complex interaction of the following interventions:

- Skin inspection, skin cleansing, care for dry skin, use of moisture barriers, and massage

- Improvement in positioning, transferring, and turning techniques to reduce skin injury caused by friction and shear forces

- Continued focus on increasing or maintaining patient activity or mobility

- Staff education programs

Universal Protocol

UP 1: The Organization Fulfills the Expectations Set Forth in the Universal Protocol for Preventing Wrong Site, Wrong Procedure, Wrong Person Surgery™ and Associated Implementation Guidelines.

Requirement 1A: Conduct a preoperative verification process, as described in the Universal Protocol.

Requirement 1B: Mark the operative site as described in the Universal Protocol.

Requirement 1C: Conduct a "time out" immediately before starting the procedure as described in the Universal Protocol.

The Universal Protocol and its requirements are applicable to ambulatory care, critical access hospitals, hospitals, and office-based surgery.

Many organizations have put forth great effort to initiate, build awareness about, and implement the Universal Protocol. Still, some organizations continue to struggle with the following areas of the Universal Protocol:

- The mark must be made using a marker that is sufficiently permanent to remain visible **after** completion of the skin preparation. Adhesive site markers should not be used as the sole means of marking the site.

- The person performing the procedure should do the site marking (while involving the patient).

- The verification process should take place at many points preoperatively, including (1) at the time the surgery/procedure is scheduled, (2) at the time of admission or entry into the facility, (3) anytime the patient is transferred to another caregiver, and (4) before the patient leaves the preoperative area or enters the operating room. Whenever possible, the verification process should also involve the patient.

- A time-out is taken immediately before starting the procedure to assure the team that they have the correct person, procedure, and site. A time out cannot take place in the preoperative holding area or hallway. Some organizations place a reminder sticker on each disposable procedure pack to remind the staff to initiate the time out before starting the procedure.

- Misinformation or errors in paperwork can potentially lead to a wrong-site procedure. To improve the information gathering part of the protocol, staff members should review and cross-check patient paperwork to clarify incorrect or missing information.

Organizations can find more information about the Universal Protocol at the Joint Commission Web site (http://www.jointcommission.org/ PatientSafety/UniversalProtocol).

Additional Information about the 2006 National Patient Safety Goals

The Joint Commission has posted on its Web site implementation expectations for the 2006 National Patient Safety Goals. The rationales and program-specific implementation expectations help organizations better understand the

2006 National Patient Safety Goals and requirements, as well as how the goals and requirements specifically relate to their organization.

The complete list of rationales and implementation expectations is available at http://www.jointcommission.org/PatientSafety/NationalPatientSafetyGoals.

What is Next?

Each year, new recommendations from *Sentinel Event Alert* newsletters published in the previous year and from other sources will be added to the pool. The Sentinel Event Advisory Group will re-evaluate the goals and requirements, and will recommend modifications, additions, or deletions to the goals and requirements for the next year. The Advisory Group's recommendations for annual National Patient Safety Goals and associated requirements are forwarded to the Joint Commission's Board of Commissioners for approval before the year in which they are to be implemented.

The proposed goals for 2007 are currently in development. Please refer to *Joint Commission Perspectives* for current information about the status of the 2007 goals.

Frequently Asked Questions about the National Patient Safety Goals

As the goals have been revised and supplemented for 2006, the Joint Commission has received a number of questions regarding applicability, implementation, and compliance. Following are some frequently asked questions and answers.

Note: *The Joint Commission regularly reviews the FAQs and updates them as necessary. Please refer to http://www.jointcommission.org/PatientSafety/NationalPatientSafetyGoals.*

Q: To what extent is an accredited organization accountable for implementation of the goals by "outside" individuals or other organizations that provide services to the accredited organization and its patients?

A: In situations in which the accredited organization cannot directly influence the actions of the "outside" individual, service, or organization, the accredited organization must, at a minimum, inform that entity about the relevant requirements of the goals and encourage their compliance with those requirements. For example, this "inform and encourage" approach is applicable to accredited health care networks with respect to their unaccredited components or to accredited freestanding pharmacies with respect to prescribing practitioners who are not employed by the pharmacy. It is not applicable to members of a hospital's medical staff when providing care to the hospital's patients. In this situation, the hospital is accountable for compliance with the National Patient Safety Goal requirements by the members of its medical staff and other independent practitioners granted privileges to provide care to patients in the organization.

Questions about Goal #2 (Communication)

Q: What is the official "do not use" list and where did it come from?

A: The "do not use" list, originally introduced by the Joint Commission in 2004, was created as part of the requirements for meeting NPSG Requirement 2B. This list was reaffirmed by participants at the National Summit on Medical Abbreviations, as well as by the health care field through a field review that covered current and new Joint Commission requirements, as well as potential additions to the list. (The list is available at http://www.jointcommission.org/PatientSafety/NationalPatientSafetyGoals.)

Q: What is the expectation for clarifying orders that contain "do not use" abbreviations?

A: Any time an order is unclear, it must be clarified with the ordering practitioner. This is an explicit requirement of the Medication Management standards (MM.3.20, EP #5 and MM.4.10, EP #6) and is addressed more broadly for other types of orders in the Leadership standards (LD.3.60, EP #2). The same requirements apply in the case of orders containing "do not use" abbreviations. That is, nurses and pharmacists exercise discretion to determine when an order is not clear and, in such cases, must contact the practitioner for clarification.

Q: There used to be an expectation that *all* orders containing "do not use" abbreviations must be clarified with the prescriber before implementing the order. Why was this expectation changed?

A: While all the terms on the Official "Do Not Use" List have been associated with misinterpretation resulting in medical errors and patient harm, the intended meaning of such a term in the context of a specific, individual order may or may not be clear and, therefore, may or may not require clarification by the prescriber. The requirement to eliminate the use of these terms is a significant and difficult change for many prescribers. Even with the best intentions and efforts, there will be occasional slips. For organizations in which there continues to be frequent use of prohibited abbreviations, the result has been a significant additional burden on nursing and pharmacy staff, reaction by some prescribers to what they perceive as unnecessary calls, and an unintended consequence of disrupted interdisciplinary collaboration and decreased responsiveness by prescribers to calls, especially from the pharmacy, leading to increased risk for patients.

Q: What can we do if some of our prescribers are unable or unwilling to stop using these prohibited terms or are unresponsive to calls from the pharmacy or other organization staff?

A: These are matters to be addressed and resolved by the medical staff. Organization leadership should work with its medical staff to eliminate the use of prohibited abbreviations. Nurses' and pharmacists' responses to the use of prohibited abbreviations should be guided by patient safety considerations, not by an assigned responsibility for monitoring and modifying prescriber behavior. It is not the responsibility of nurses or pharmacists to manage the behaviors of prescribers. Joint Commission standards assign to the medical staff the responsibility for overseeing the quality and safety of patient care, treatment, and services provided by practitioners privileged through the medical staff process and, in particular, providing leadership in activities related to patient safety and improving performance associated with significant

departures from established patterns of clinical practice.

Q: What is the impact of this change on scoring this safety goal or related standards?

A: This change in expectations for clarification of orders containing "do not use" abbreviations does not affect the scoring of NPSG requirement 2B. The scoring of this requirement has been and will continue to be based only on the actual use of the prohibited terms. Failure to contact the prescriber when there are concerns, issues, or questions about an order will be scored at MM.4.10 (EP #6) for medication orders or at LD.3.60 (EP #2) for other types of orders. Failure of the medical staff to exercise its responsibilities for oversight of the actions of practitioners privileged through the medical staff process is scored at standards MS.2.10 and MS.3.10.

Q: Are there any monitoring requirements associated with this expectation for clarifying orders that not clear?

A: Medication Management standard MM.8.10 and the Improving Organization Performance standards require measurement, assessment, and improvement activities related to identified risk points. The decision on which processes and risk points are to be monitored is left to the organization. However, because the accuracy of orders is so crucial to patient safety, organizations are encouraged to monitor implementation of their processes for responding to unclear orders.

Q: For the "timeliness" requirements (2C and 2D), is the Joint Commission going to determine the length of time?

A: No. The Joint Commission expects an organization to define the acceptable length of time: a) between the ordering of critical tests and reporting the test results and values, and b) between the availability of critical results and receipt by the responsible licensed caregiver.

Q: Is it true that use of a "trailing zero" is allowed for laboratory values and equipment sizes?

A: Yes, although the "trailing zero" is still prohibited for all medication orders and other medication-related documentation. In reporting laboratory values and in certain other numeric notations, the precision of the numeric value is indicated by the digits after the decimal point, even when that trailing digit is a zero. For example, a serum potassium level might be reported as 4.0 mEq/Liter, not 4 mEq/Liter. Similarly, sizes for endotracheal tubes and other clinical equipment are often specified numerically with one place after the decimal point. This is acceptable, even when the number after the decimal point is a zero.

Q: In a home care service, physicians or their agents frequently leave orders on nurse voice mail. Is this acceptable given the NPSG requirement for read back?

A: No. Voice mail orders are not acceptable within the context of the NPSGs. Also, most state laws require nurses and pharmacists to obtain the order directly from the prescriber or his/her agent. When not received directly, the nurse or pharmacist must call the prescriber back to get the order directly, including a "read-back."

Q: In home care, there are times when the parent or other family member is the patient's primary caregiver. This leads to the family member receiving verbal or telephone orders from physicians when there is no nurse in the home at the time, then communicating the orders to the nurse when she arrives. Is this acceptable?

A: Patients or their family members are not considered physicians' agents, nor are they qualified by law and regulation in most (if not all) states to receive orders for care. If, in a particular locality, this is legally permissible, then a "read-back" of any verbal or telephone order should be carried out, and the family member would have to be trained to do this.

Questions About Goal #3

Q: What is the Joint Commission's position regarding the Broselow Tape, the Rule of Six, and the requirement under NPSG #3 for limiting and standardizing drug concentrations in health care organizations that provide neonatal and pediatric care services?

A: The Joint Commission recently learned that some of its surveyors have mistakenly

told hospitals that they were not in compliance with NPSG #3B if they continued to have Broselow Tapes in their crash carts. This is not the Joint Commission's position. The only issue with the Broselow tape is that one of its functions is to support a method for mixing customized (patient-specific) concentrations rather than using standardized concentrations. Unlike other applications of the "Rule of 6," which require calculation of these different concentrations, the Broselow Tape gives the concentrations without the need for calculations.

The Broselow Tape is a multi-purpose aid in the emergency care of children. In that regard, the Joint Commission recognizes the usefulness of the tape in quickly identifying appropriate equipment sizes and doses of medications with standardized concentrations. Even if the organization is already using standardized concentrations, it may continue to use the Broselow Tape for its other functions. The confusion has arisen in the context of the Joint Commission's requirement that all hospitals move to standardized concentrations of drugs by 2008. For organizations that are not already using standardized concentrations, a transitional period has been provided. During this transition to standardized concentrations, if the organization has been using the Rule of 6 and the Broselow Tape is part of its system, then it may continue to use it for that purpose during the transition as long as it has submitted and received approval of a Request for Review of an Alternative Approach to the NPSG and is complying with the criteria for transitioning from the Rule of 6 to standardized concentrations.

Questions About Goal #7 (Reducing Infections)

Q: What is the Joint Commission's position on the length of staff members' fingernails and the use of artificial fingernails with respect to infection control?

A: Through goal 7, the Joint Commission requires organizations to comply with the CDC's hand hygiene guidelines. These guidelines include specific recommendations that state that staff who provide direct care to "high-risk patients" (intensive care unit patients, immunocompromised patients, and so forth) should not wear artificial fingernails and should keep finger-nails trimmed to less than one-quarter inch.

Each of the CDC's recommendations carry a notation regarding the strength of evidence supporting the recommendation: Category I or Category II evidence. As part of goal 7, the Joint Commission requires compliance with all the recommendations that have Category I evidence and recommends compliance with Category II recommenda-tions. "Artificial fingernails" is a Category I recommendation; one-quarter inch nails is a Category II recommendation.

Q: Do organizations have to use alcohol-based hand cleaners?

A: Accredited organizations are required to provide health care workers with a readily accessible alcohol-based hand rub product (CDC recommendations 8 C&D). However, use of an alcohol-based hand rub cleaner by any individual health care worker is not required.

The guidelines describe when this type of cleaner may be used instead of soap and water. If a staff member chooses not to use it, then soap and water should be used instead.

For additional questions about the National Patient Safety Goals, please contact the Standards Interpretation Group at 630/792-5900, or complete the Standards Online Question Submission Form at http://www.jointcommission.org/Standards/OnlineQuestionForm.

References

1. Rozich J.D.: "Standardization as a mechanism to improve safety and health care." *Jt Comm J Qual Saf* 30(1):5–11, 2004.

PART II

Safety Standards and the Accreditation Process

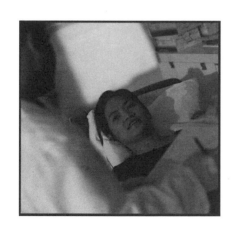
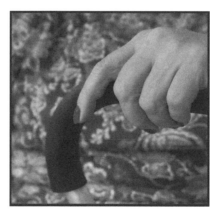
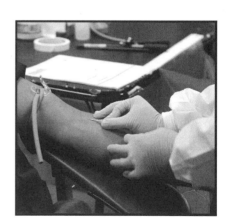

CHAPTER THREE

Patient Safety Standards: A Look at Joint Commission Requirements

Introduction to Patient Safety Standards

The Joint Commission's safety standards are designed to improve patient safety and to reduce risk to patients. Recognizing that effective health care risk reduction requires an integrated and coordinated approach, the following standards expand and emphasize safety as a major focus of accreditation, and pertain specifically to leadership's role in an organizationwide safety program that includes all activities within the organization which contribute to the maintenance and improvement of patient safety, such as performance improvement, environmental safety, infection control, and risk management.

The standards do not require the creation of new structures or "offices" within the organization; rather, the standards emphasize the need to integrate all patient-safety activities, both existing and newly created, with an identified locus of accountability within the organization's leadership.

Note: *The original term safety standards arose in 2001 when the Joint Commission added several new standards to complement standards addressing patient safety that were already in the accreditation manuals. These safety standards were intended to expand and emphasize safety as a major focus of accreditation; these are the standards that are discussed in this chapter. It is important to clarify, however, that these standards apply to all health care providers within an organization, not just one person, such as a patient safety coordinator or a risk manager. It is also important to point out that the majority of Joint Commission standards do directly address patient safety.*

Although the standards focus on patient safety, it would be difficult to create an organizationwide safety initiative that excludes staff and visitors. Furthermore, many of the activities taken to improve patient safety (such as security, equipment safety, and infection control) encompass staff and visitors as well as patients.

Effective reduction of factors that contribute to unanticipated adverse events and/or outcomes in a health care organization requires an environment in which patients, their families, and organization staff and leaders can identify and manage actual and potential risks to patient safety. This environment encourages the following concepts:

- Recognition and acknowledgment of risks and unanticipated adverse events and the initiation of actions to reduce these risks

- The internal reporting of what has been found and the actions taken

- A focus on processes and systems

- Minimization of individual blame or retribution for involvement in an unanticipated adverse event

- Organization learning about medical/health care error

- Sharing of knowledge and information to effect behavioral changes within an organization as well as within other health care organizations to improve patient safety

Organization leaders are responsible for fostering such an environment through their personal example and by establishing mechanisms that support effective responses to actual occurrences; ongoing proactive reduction of unanticipated adverse events; and integration of patient safety priorities into the new design and redesign of all relevant organization processes, functions, and services.

All safety standards for ambulatory care, behavioral health care, critical access hospital, hospital, and long term care organizations and office-based surgery practices appear in Matrix 1 beginning on page 74 of this chapter; all safety standards for home care organizations appear in Matrix 2, beginning on page 97. In addition, because several safety standards do not apply to all ambulatory care settings, the matrix in Figure 3-1, page 114, displays which ambulatory care safety standards apply to which ambulatory care settings.

Safety Standards: What the Requirements Mean

Integrating the patient safety standards into an organization's daily operations does not have to be intimidating. The changes do not necessitate new departments, structures, or staff, but instead emphasize the integration of safety activities into existing processes. First, organization leaders should review the functions that will be affected and make sure they understand the requirements. Then, they should look for ways to integrate these requirements into their existing processes to create a coordinated, organizationwide, and proactive patient safety program.

Although safety and risk management have always been implicit in the Joint Commission's standards, the safety standards put these issues at the forefront of leadership, staff, and patient/family awareness. They complement previously existing safety-related requirements, introducing or strengthening concepts derived from the lessons learned in the Joint Commission's ongoing review of sentinel events and from other high-risk fields. Standards that address improving patient safety and reducing unanticipated adverse events appear in several functional chapters, but the strongest focus is on leaders' responsibility to build an environment that recognizes the importance of these goals.

Ethics, Rights, and Responsibilities

The safety standard in the "Ethics, Rights, and Responsibilities"* (RI) chapter requires that a licensed independent practitioner or another caregiver responsible for a patient's care should explain all outcomes of care, including any unexpected outcomes of that care, to the

patient/family. This standard specifically includes unanticipated outcomes that relate to sentinel events that are considered reviewable by the Joint Commission. In behavioral health care settings, if there is no licensed independent practitioner, the staff member responsible for the client's care is responsible for sharing information about outcomes. In home care settings, the person responsible for explaining outcomes should be someone who understands the scope and significance of the outcome and is capable of answering any questions the patient or family might have.

Many organizations have asked the Joint Commission what this standard *doesn't* require. It does not require organizations to inform patients about errors that occurred in the course of their care, nor does it require organizations to identify how or why an error occurred. It also does not require organizations to identify who committed an error, and it does not require any specific documentation. However, organizations should establish what will be communicated to their patients beyond the minimum requirement of informing their patients about the outcomes of their care. *See* Sidebar 3-1 on page 63 for practical strategies for disclosing errors.

Improving Organization Performance

One safety standard found in the "Improving Organization Performance"† (PI) chapter that was previously in the "Leadership" (LD) chapter requires organizations to implement an ongoing, proactive program for identifying risks to patients and reducing adverse outcomes and events; this program involves performing ongoing measurement and periodic analysis of at least one high-risk, error-prone process to determine whether performance varies from what is intended. For example, in an ambulatory care setting, the areas of surgical site identification, medication management, medical gas storage, and transfusion processes should all be examined because they contain areas of high risk. For behavioral health care organizations, one of the highest risks in foster care is accurate, adequate screening of foster families. If a relatively high number of placements have not worked

---

* This chapter is titled "Practice Ethics, and Patient Rights and Responsibilities" in the *Accreditation Manual for Office-Based Surgery Practices*, 2nd edition.

† This chapter is titled "Improving Practice Performance" in the *Accreditation Manual for Office-Based Surgery Practices*, 2nd edition.

Sidebar 3-1. Communication Strategies for Disclosing Errors

Talking honestly with the patient and his or her family following an adverse event is critical but is not always easy. The hurdles are numerous and very real. One hurdle is helping staff to feel as comfortable as possible with the conversation. A nonpunitive environment is key. Staff must feel supported in talking with colleagues and the patient and family about the outcome of care including, if consistent with organization policy, any errors. Communication strategies can include the following:

• Meet with the care team to review the event's factual details and to reconcile differing perceptions.

• Consider who should be part of the communication team.

• Designate a spokesperson (usually the physician in charge of the patient's care).

• Meet with the patient and family as soon as possible after the event's occurrence, in a quiet, private space.

• Accurately describe the patient's current condition and prognosis, using nontechnical, understandable language.

• Provide a factual explanation, not speculation, of what happened.

• Express sincere sympathy and compassion. Statements such as "I'm sorry this happened" demonstrate a caring attitude.

• Answer questions factually, and when the facts are not yet clear, focus only on outcomes.

• Do not accept blame by criticizing yourself or assign blame by criticizing other providers.

• Leave the door open for further communication. Identify the person whom family members can contact when they have additional questions.

• During follow-up conversations, describe how the event is being studied and what changes are being made to prevent recurrence.

out, organizations might want to review their screening methods. For home care organizations, a comprehensive risk assessment of the home itself could result in a decrease in falls, reduction of fire risk, and reduced likelihood of self-inflicted injury. A long term care organization with a high fall rate might want to measure and assess completion of the falls-risk assessment by staff. Examining this process might result in improving staff education or redesigning the falls protocol.

Proactively identifying and managing potential risks have the obvious advantage of preventing adverse occurrences rather than simply causing staff to react when they do occur. This approach also avoids the fear of disclosure, embarrassment, blame, and punishment that can arise in the wake of a sentinel event.

The PI standards also require organizations to address safety issues when collecting data to monitor performance. Information should be collected from patients and families regarding how the organization can improve safety and their perceptions of risk. Some ways to collect patient and family data are to include questions about safety and risks in the following:

■ Postdischarge satisfaction surveys

■ The discharge planning process

■ Routine postdischarge follow-up calls

Information should also be collected from staff about their willingness to report errors, opinions about risk, and suggestions for improvement. Ways to collect this information include the following:

■ Offer a brief, anonymous questionnaire in a tear-out-and-mail-back portion of organizationwide newsletters

■ Insert such questionnaires into paycheck envelopes

■ Offer safety queries as preliminary intranet screens

■ Provide voice mailboxes that do not reveal a person's identity

■ Establish public-access computers placed in the staff cafeteria for obtaining anonymous information

Organizations should analyze all suggestions and perceptions collected to identify system changes that will improve performance and patient safety. Organizations should implement changes on a test basis to make necessary revisions on a small scale. After revisions occur, changes can be implemented organizationwide and monitored to ensure ongoing effectiveness in enhancing safety. In addition, undesirable patterns or trends should also be analyzed.

Leadership

Standards requirements in the "Leadership"[*] (LD) function require organization leaders to consider safety when designing processes,

---

[*] This chapter is titled "Practice Leadership" in the *Accreditation Manual for Office-Based Surgery Practices*, 2nd edition.

functions, or services. Good process design aimed at minimizing the likelihood of process or system failures should incorporate available information from internal and external sources about potential risks to patients and successful practices.

The safety standards in the LD chapter also address how leaders can ensure that safety is a high priority in their health care organizations. Leaders need to allocate financial, informational, physical, and human resources to improvement activities in patient safety and regularly evaluate whether these resources are adequate. In addition, leaders need to evaluate how effective their own performance has been in organizationwide efforts to improve patient safety. Leaders also need to work with the directors of relevant departments and encourage communication and cooperation among all staff to implement ways to improve patient safety.

The LD safety standards also highlight leadership's responsibility in fostering a safe environment throughout the organization by integrating safety priorities into all relevant organization processes, functions, and services. Such an organizationwide safety program should include all activities that contribute to maintaining and improving patient safety, such as performance improvement (PI), environmental safety, infection control, and risk management. These standards are not meant to require the creation of new structures or offices within the organization. Rather, they emphasize the need to coordinate all patient safety activities, both existing and new, with accountability resting with the organization's leadership. For example, if the staff members who manage the environment of care discover a medical equipment problem that could compromise patient safety, they need to communicate it to those involved in managing the patient safety program.

To that end, the standards call for an integrated patient safety program managed by one or more qualified individuals or an interdisciplinary group. Typically, individuals involved could include representatives from the major clinical disciplines, administration, the PI coordinator, and possibly a risk manager. The program should also define the types of general occurrences to be addressed, ranging from harmless slips on the floor to sentinel events.

The program should also indicate the following:

- Procedures for immediately responding to system or process failures, including caring for the affected patient(s), containing risk to others, and preserving factual information for subsequent analysis

- Clear systems for internal and external reporting of information about system or process failures

- Defined responses to various types of adverse occurrences and processes for conducting proactive risk assessment/ risk reduction activities

- Defined support systems for staff members who have been involved in sentinel events

The organization's governing body or other authority should be informed, at least annually, about the occurrence of system or process failures and the actions taken to improve patient safety. This report should address both proactive activities and those that occurred in response to actual events.

Management of the Environment of Care

The safety standards found within the "Management of the Environment of Care"[*] (EC) chapter require organizations to do the following:

- Collect information about deficiencies and opportunities for improvement in the care environment

- Analyze identified environmental issues and develop recommendations for resolving them

- Implement recommendations to improve the environment and monitor the effectiveness of the recommendations' implementation

As a group, the safety-related EC standards clarify how organizations can integrate

---

[*] This chapter is titled "Environmental Safety and Equipment Management" in the *2006-2007 Comprehensive Accreditation Manual for Home Care (CAMHC)*.

existing safety functions and initiatives to meet patient safety requirements. Organizations need to link how they assess, improve, and monitor the effectiveness of relevant environmental safety issues within the required organizationwide patient safety program. Responsibility for this integration should belong to an individual or a group assigned by the organization's leaders. This individual or group must direct ongoing, organizationwide collection of information about deficiencies in and opportunities for improvement in the environment of care. This information includes environmental risks, failures, accidents, and incidents involving such areas as the following:

- Safety

- Security

- Hazardous materials and waste

- Emergency management

- Life safety

- Utility systems

- Equipment management

- Other environmental considerations

The individual or group must also report on findings, recommendations, actions taken, and results of measurement; regularly participate in hazard surveillance and incident reporting; and participate in the development of safety policies and procedures.

Note that in some facilities, the individual(s) responsible for patient safety may or may not be the same person responsible for overseeing EC issues. However, each individual responsible for safety, regardless of whether it is EC safety or patient safety, must communicate and coordinate with his or her counterpart.

Management of Human Resources

Within the "Management of Human Resources" (HR) function, initiatives such as orientation, ongoing in-services/continuing education, and team training should emphasize specific safety-related aspects of each job. Multidisciplinary participation and support are necessary to incorporate a safety focus into daily activities. Orientation and ongoing training of both full-time employees and volunteers should include both the safety program as a whole and any aspects specific to individual positions.

To ensure patient safety and prevent sentinel events, organization leaders must prioritize staff orientation and training and must support such programs with appropriate resources and funding. Leaders need to pay special attention to teaching staff about patient safety at orientation—before staff members have contact with or provide care, treatment, and services to patients. It is important, too, to cover patient safety issues with all full-time and part-time staff during organization, department, and job-specific orientation—not just with staff who provide direct patient care. Organizations should include volunteers, medical staff, contracted staff, temporary (agency) staff, float staff, housekeeping, and maintenance staff—basically anyone who provides care, treatment, and services or supports those activities. Patient safety should be an organizationwide goal, achieved only with the involvement and collaboration of all individuals working in the organization.

Organizations do not need to develop a separate orientation program or separate in-services specifically for patient safety. It can be included in general, departmental, and job-specific orientation programs and in-services. The orientation and training processes should explain at least the following, as appropriate to the job responsibilities of the staff being trained:

- Specific job duties

- Safety issues specific to individual job assignments

- Life safety procedures

- Infection control practices

- Organization, department, and individual staff procedures for preventing fires, utility system failures, and other emergencies

- Systems for internal and external reporting of information about errors

- Mechanisms for support of staff who have been involved in a sentinel event, including reassurance that the organization wants to improve systems, not blame individuals, when examining sentinel or other adverse events

- The organization's mission and values

- The organization's PI program

- "Hot" patient safety topics relevant to the organization, such as medication errors, patient suicide, infant abduction, restraint and seclusion, and patient falls; organizations should provide staff with strategies and resources to deal with these issues

Depending on the type of organization, orientation may include other information that pertains directly to patient safety. For example, staff in long term care organizations should be informed about the organization's EC management plans, accident prevention, resident rights and responsibilities, and policies and criteria for identifying and handling victims of abuse. Long term care organizations must also orient new hires about the special needs of their resident population(s) and how to provide residents with appropriate care.

In home care and hospice settings, orientation should specifically address patient safety issues such as the following:

- Emergency preparedness and appropriate actions to be taken in unsafe situations

- Storing, handling, and accessing supplies, medical gases, and drugs

- Managing equipment

- Identifying, handling, and disposing of hazardous or infectious materials and waste

- Evaluating safety issues in the home

Management of Information

Organizations must identify barriers to effective communication and develop processes for ensuring accurate, timely, and complete verbal and written communication among caregivers and all others involved in using data. The safety standards in the "Management of Information" (IM) chapter require organizations to effectively manage information through the use of uniform data definitions; standardized lists of abbreviations, acronyms, and symbols not to be used; quality control systems; storage and retrieval systems; and so forth. Organizations' information management processes should support managerial and operational decisions; performance improvement activities; and patient care, treatment, and service decisions.

In addition, organizations' knowledge-based information management systems must support risk reduction activities and include collection and aggregation of data pertaining to safety risks. Organizations' knowledge-based information should also support PI and patient safety activities.

Tips for Continuous Patient Safety Standards Compliance

Organizations should consider the following tips when planning how to implement the safety standards:

- Integrate the standards requirements into existing committees. The patient safety standards do not require the creation of any new organization structures.

- Consider sentinel event and near miss RCA information when deciding which safety-related improvement projects to initiate

- Include safety risks and suggestions for improving safety in surveys of staff and patient perceptions

- Consider recommendations published in issues of *Sentinel Event Alert* (http://www.jointcommission.org/ SentinelEvents/SentinelEventAlert) as starting points for safety initiatives

- Measure and analyze data related to error-prone processes identified for proactive risk-reduction activities. Then apply this information to appropriate corrective actions and the process redesign step(s) to enhance safety systems.

- Reanalyze and pilot-test all new or revised safety improvement process designs before implementing them

The Joint Commission's Sentinel Event Policy: The Relation to Safety

Despite an organization's efforts at proactive risk assessment, sentinel events can still occur. As difficult as dealing with a sentinel event can be, organizations can turn these events into learning experiences. By identifying root causes of a sentinel event and developing processes to prevent recurrence, organizations can limit sentinel events and thus improve overall patient safety. Despite every organization's unique qualities, most sentinel events have causes that might be relevant to other organizations. By sharing information, organizations can learn how others have dealt with similar problems and what policies and procedures were put in place to prevent future occurrences.

The Joint Commission defines a sentinel event as an unexpected occurrence involving death or serious physical—including loss of limb or function—or psychological injury, or the risk thereof. "Risk thereof" means that, although no harm occurred this time, any recurrence would carry a significant chance of a serious adverse outcome.

The Joint Commission's Sentinel Event Policy requires that any time a sentinel event occurs, health care organizations must complete a thorough and credible root cause analysis (RCA), implement improvements to reduce risk, and monitor the effectiveness of those improvements. The RCA is expected to drill down to underlying organization systems and processes that can be altered to reduce the likelihood of a failure in the future and to protect patients from harm when a failure does occur. The policy also encourages organizations to report to the Joint Commission any sentinel events that resulted in death or serious injury, along with their root causes and related preventive actions, so that the Joint Commission can learn about the underlying causes of the sentinel events, share lessons learned with other health care organizations, and reduce the risk of future sentinel event occurrences. Sidebar 3-2, "Why Organizations Should Report Sentinel Events," above right, provides rationale for reporting sentinel events.

Reviewable sentinel events include events that have resulted in an unanticipated death or major permanent loss of function, not

---

Sidebar 3-2. Why Organizations Should Report Sentinel Events

Although the Joint Commission does not require accredited health care organizations to report sentinel events, doing so has the following advantages:

- All health care organizations will benefit from knowing basic information about other organizations' sentinel events. When an organization reports a sentinel event, the information about the type, setting, outcome, and root cause of the sentinel event is added to the Joint Commission's Sentinel Event Database. That shared information contributes to the general knowledge about sentinel events and to the reduction of risk for such events in many other organizations.

- Organizations can collaborate with the Joint Commission during the development of the root cause analysis and action plan.

- Organizations publicize their culture of safety by letting the public know that they are doing everything possible to ensure that such an event will not happen again.

---

related to the natural course of the patient's illness or underlying condition, **or** the event is one of the following (even if the outcome was not death or major permanent loss of function, not related to the natural course of the patient's illness or underlying condition) (recent additions to this list are underlined):

- Suicide <u>of any individual receiving care in a staffed around-the-clock care setting or within 72 hours of discharge</u>

- Unanticipated death of a full-term infant

- <u>Abduction of any individual receiving care</u>

- Discharge of an infant to the wrong family

- Rape

- Hemolytic transfusion reaction involving administration of blood or blood products having major blood group incompatibilities

- Surgery on the wrong patient or wrong body part

- Unintended retention of a foreign object in a patient after surgery or other procedure

- <u>Severe neonatal hyperbilirubinemia (bilirubin >30 milligrams/deciliter)</u>

- <u>Prolonged fluoroscopy with cumulative dose >1500 rads to a single field or any delivery of radiotherapy to the wrong body region or >25% above the planned radiotherapy dose</u>

Sentinel Events and the Safety Standards

The Joint Commission has been working closely with health care organizations to identify potential sentinel events, learn about their root causes, and implement proactive risk reduction strategies. The Joint Commission's latest work in this effort resulted in the safety standards in the LD and PI chapters. The LD standard requires each accredited organization to define sentinel event for its own purposes in order to establish mechanisms to identify, report, and manage these events. While this definition must be consistent with the general definition of sentinel event published by the Joint Commission, accredited organizations have some latitude in setting more specific parameters to define *unexpected, serious,* and *the risk thereof.* At a minimum, an organization's definition must include those events subject to review under the Sentinel Event Policy as defined in the accreditation manuals.

Expectations for an Organization's Response to a Sentinel Event

To comply with the safety standards and the Sentinel Event Policy, accredited organizations are expected to identify and respond appropriately to all sentinel events (as defined by the organization in accordance with the preceding paragraph) occurring in the organization or associated with services that the organization provides, or provides for. Appropriate responses include the following:

■ Conducting a timely, thorough, and credible root cause analysis

■ Developing an action plan designed to implement improvements to reduce risk. Such a plan should address responsibility for implementation, oversight, pilot-testing as appropriate, time lines, and strategies for measuring the effectiveness of the actions.

■ Implementing the improvements

■ Monitoring the effectiveness of those improvements

In addition, the Joint Commission recently implemented the following revisions to its Sentinel Event Policy. These revisions are applicable to organizations that fail to submit an RCA by the RCA "due date" (within 45 calendar days of the known occurrence of the event):

■ If the organization has failed to submit an RCA within an additional thirty (30) days following its RCA due date, its accreditation status will automatically be changed to Provisional Accreditation, and both the organization and the Accreditation Committee will be so notified. **This provision replaces Accreditation Watch.**

■ If the organization has failed to submit an RCA within sixty (60) days following its RCA due date, its accreditation status will automatically be changed to Conditional Accreditation, and both the organization and the Accreditation Committee will be so notified.

■ If the organization then continues to fail to submit an RCA for ninety (90) days following its RCA due date, a recommendation for Denial of Accreditation will be presented to the Accreditation Committee. The organization would then be given the opportunity to submit a response to the Accreditation Committee. However, if the Committee were to reach a Denial of Accreditation decision, the organization would not have access to the appeals process.

Acceptability of RCA and Action Plans

The acceptability criteria for an RCA and action plan are listed under the "Review of Root Cause Analyses and Action Plans" section in the "Sentinel Events" chapter of the accreditation manuals. Under the revised process, if the RCA and action plan are not acceptable but were received within the stipulated time frame, Joint Commission staff will provide consultative support to the organization and allow an additional 15 days for submission of an acceptable RCA and action plan. The following revisions are applicable to organizations that fail to submit an acceptable revised RCA and action plan:

■ If the revised RCA and/or action plan continue to be unacceptable, the organization's accreditation status will automatically be changed to Provisional Accreditation, and both the organization and the Accreditation Committee will be so notified. Joint

Commission staff will provide additional consultation to the organization and allow an additional 10 business days for the organization to submit an acceptable RCA and action plan. The organization's accreditation status reverts to Accredited when the RCA and action plan are determined to be acceptable.

- If the third submission continues to be unacceptable, staff will recommend that the organization's accreditation status be changed to Conditional Accreditation, and both the organization and the Accreditation Committee will be so notified. The organization will have one final 45-day period in which to submit an acceptable RCA and action plan.

Follow-Up Activity

The follow-up activity—now titled "Sentinel Event Measure of Success" (SE MOS)—is due 4 months after the RCA and action plan are determined to be acceptable. The following bullet points outline the SE MOS requirement:

- If the SE MOS is 60 or more days late, staff will recommend that the organization's accreditation status be changed to Conditional Accreditation, and both the organization and the Accreditation Committee will be so notified.

- If the SE MOS is submitted on time but is found to be unacceptable, staff will request an additional 4 months of data, the organization's accreditation status will be changed to Provisional Accreditation, and both the organization and the Accreditation Committee will be so notified.

- If the second set of data is acceptable, the organization's Accredited status will be restored.

- If the second set of data is found to be unacceptable, Joint Commission staff will recommend that the organization's accreditation status be changed to Conditional Accreditation, and both the organization and the Accreditation Committee will be so notified. Any further actions will be based on the standards-based MOS decision rules.

For definitions of each accreditation decision category, please see Chapter 5, page 155.

Sentinel Event Alert: The Link to Safety

The Joint Commission has been publishing *Sentinel Event Alert* since February 1998. This free, periodic, e-mail newsletter identifies particular sentinel events, describes their common underlying causes, and provides recommendations for reducing risks of recurrence. Information for *Sentinel Event Alert* comes predominantly from the Joint Commission's sentinel events database, as well as from experts and other organizations. The Joint Commission's database includes the sentinel events that have been reported to the Joint Commission, the root causes of these events, and strategies that health care organizations have used to reduce risks to patients. The Joint Commission began publishing *Sentinel Event Alert* to share the lessons learned from its database and to provide important information about the occurrence and management of sentinel events in health care organizations.

Since its creation, *Sentinel Event Alert* has raised awareness in the health care community and the federal government about the occurrence of adverse events and ways that these events can be prevented in the future. Past issues of this publication are available on the Joint Commission's Web site, http://www.jointcommission.org/ SentinelEvents/SentinelEventAlert.

Using Sentinel Event Alert in Safety Improvement Efforts

By distributing *Sentinel Event Alert*, the Joint Commission encourages organizations to implement the suggestions found within the publication to prevent errors and enhance patient safety.

Currently, during the on-site survey of accredited organizations, Joint Commission surveyors assess, for educational purposes, the organization's familiarity with and use of *Sentinel Event Alert* information. Accredited organizations are expected to do the following:

- Review and consider relevant information from each *Alert*, if appropriate to the organization's services

- Consider information in an *Alert* when designing or redesigning relevant processes

- Evaluate systems in light of information in an *Alert*

- Consider implementing relevant suggestions or reasonable alternatives

While the Joint Commission expects organizations to review the *Alerts* and implement the recommendations that are relevant to the services they provide, only those recommendations that are associated with the National Patient Safety Goals are actually surveyed and scored. During the survey, surveyors may discuss recommendations published in *Alerts* as suggestions for improvement, but implementation of those recommendations will not be assessed.

Safety Standards Matrix

The standards presented in matrix format on the following pages are the common standards for patient safety. The matrixes identify where variations for each setting occur.

Note 1: *An additional matrix for ambulatory care organizations appears in Figure 3-1, pages 114–118. This matrix identifies which ambulatory care safety standards apply to which ambulatory care settings.*

Note 2: *Some safety standards for behavioral health care organizations do not apply to all behavioral health care programs and services. Exceptions are noted in Matrix 1.*

Note 3: *Different settings use different language. For Matrix 1, the following terms will be used:*

Patient—also refers to client or resident

Organization—refers to ambulatory care organization, critical access hospital, behavioral health care organization, hospital, long term care organization, or office-based surgery practice

Care—also refers to care, treatment, and services

The standards, rationales, and EPs in each program's accreditation manual are the final arbiters to be assessed during the accreditation process.

A **measure of success** icon—**Ⓜ**—appears next to some EPs. Measures of success (MOS) need to be developed for certain EPs when a standard is judged to be out of compliance through either the Periodic Performance Review (PPR) or the onsite survey. An MOS is defined as a quantifiable measure, usually related to an audit, that can be used to determine whether an action has been effective and is being sustained.

Using the Self-Assessment Grid to Assess Your Compliance

Two components are scored for each EP: (1) compliance with the requirement itself and (2) compliance with the track record* for that requirement. Scoring has been simplified and track record achievements (which have always been part of the scoring) have been appropriately modified.

Note: Some standards and EPs do not apply to a particular type of organization; these standards and EPs are marked "not applicable" and the related text is not included. Your organization is not expected to comply with standards and EPs marked "not applicable."

Step 1: Score Your Compliance with Each Element of Performance

Before you can determine your compliance with the standards, you must score your compliance with each EP. First look at the EP scoring criterion category listed immediately preceding the scoring scale in the margin next to the EP. There are three scoring criterion categories: A, B, and C (described below). Please note that for each EP scoring criterion category, your organization must meet the performance requirement itself and the track record achievements (*see* below).

---

* **Track record** The amount of time that an organization has been in compliance with a standard, element of performance, or other requirement.

Category A

These EPs relate to the presence or absence of the requirement(s) and are scored either yes (2) or no (0); however, score 1 for partial compliance is also possible based on track record achievements (*see* page 73).

If an A EP has multiple components designated by bullets, your organization must be compliant with all the bullets to receive a score of 2. If your organization does not meet one or more requirements in the bullets, you will receive a score of 0.

Category B

Category B EPs are scored in two steps:

1. As with category A EPs, category B EPs relate to the presence or absence of the requirement(s). If your organization *does not meet* the requirement(s), the EP is scored 0; there is no need to assess your compliance with the principles of good process design (*see* page 73).

2. If your organization *does meet* the requirement(s), but there is concern about the quality or comprehensiveness of the effort, then and only then should you assess the qualitative aspect of the EP. That is, review the applicable principles of good process design and ask how the principles were applied in the situation under discussion. Good process design has the following characteristics:

   • Is consistent with your organization's mission, values, and goals

   • Meets the needs of patients

   • Reflects the use of currently accepted practices (doing the right thing, using resources responsibly, using practice guidelines)

   • Incorporates current safety information and knowledge such as sentinel event data and National Patient Safety Goals

   • Incorporates relevant performance improvement results

This two-part evaluation applies to both simple and bulleted B EPs. First, the EPs are assessed to determine if the requirements are present. If the EP has multiple components designated by bullets, as with the category A EPs, your organization must meet the requirements in *all* the bulleted items to get a score of 2. If your organization meets *none* of the requirements in the bullets, it receives a score of 0. If your organization meets *at least one, but not all,* of the bulleted requirements, it will receive a score of 1 for the EPs.

Use the following rules to determine your EP score:

   • Your EP score is 0 if your organization does not meet the requirement(s); you *do not* need to assess your compliance with the preceding applicable principles of good process design

   • Your EP score is 1 if your organization does meet the requirement(s), but considered only *some* of the preceding applicable principles of good process design

   • Your EP score is 2 if your organization does meet the requirement(s) *and* considered *all* the preceding principles of good process design

Your EP score is also based on consistent implementation in all applicable situations at all times (when there is not a corresponding EP to separately score implementation of the requirement). If the requirement is applied in all applicable situations, your EP score is 2 (satisfactory compliance); if the requirement is applied in fewer than all applicable situations, your EP score is 1 (partial compliance); if the requirement is not applied in any applicable situation, your EP score is 0 (insufficient compliance).

Category C

C EPs are scored 0, 1, or 2 based on the number of times your organization does not meet the EP. These EPs are frequency based and require totaling the number of occurrences (that is, results of performance or nonperformance) related to a particular EP. Each situation discovered by a surveyor(s) will be counted as a separate occurrence.

Note: Multiple events of the same type related to a single patient and single practitioner/staff member are counted as one occurrence only.

Use the following rules to determine your EP score:

• Your EP score is 2 if you find one or fewer occurrences of noncompliance with the EP

• Your EP score is 1 if you find two occurrences of noncompliance with the EP

• Your EP score is 0 if you find three or more occurrences of noncompliance with the EP

If an EP in the C category has multiple requirements designated by bullets, the following scoring guidelines apply:

• If there are fewer than 2 findings in all bullets, the EP is scored 2

• If there are three or more findings in all bullets, the EP is scored 0

• In all other combinations of findings, the EP is scored 1

Track Record Achievements

In addition to meeting the requirement(s) in each EP, regardless of category, your organization must also meet the following track record achievements:

Score	Initial Survey	Full Survey
2	4 months or more	12 months or more
1	2 to 3 months	6 to 11 months
0	Fewer than 2 months	Fewer than 6 months

Step 2: Use Your EP Scores to Gauge Your Compliance with the Standards

Now that you have evaluated and scored each EP for a particular standard, use these simple rules to determine your compliance with the standard itself:

• Your organization is not in compliance (that is, "not compliant") with the standard if any EP is scored 0

• Otherwise, your organization is in compliance with a standard if 65% or more of its EPs are scored 2

Scoring Grid

0	Insufficient compliance
1	Partial compliance
2	Satisfactory compliance
NA	Not applicable

Elements of Performance for PI.1.10

		AMB	BHC	CAH	HAP	LTC	OBS
B [0] [1] [2] [NA]	1. The organization collects data for priorities identified by leaders (*see* standard LD.4.50 in the accreditation manual).	X	X	X	X	X	X
A [0] [1] [2] [NA]	2. The organization considers collecting data in the following areas:	X	X*	X	X	X	
	● Staff opinions and needs	X	X	X	X	X	
	● Staff perceptions of risks to individuals and suggestions for improving patient safety	X	X	X	X	X	
	● Staff willingness to report unanticipated adverse events	X	X	X	X	X	
	● Outcomes of care, treatment, and services		X				
B [0] [1] [2] [NA]	3. The organization collects data on the perceptions of care, treatment, and services* of patients, including the following:	X	X†	X	X	X	X
	● Their specific needs and expectations	X	X	X	X	X	X
	● How well the organization meets these needs and expectations	X	X	X	X	X	X
	● How the organization can improve patient safety	X	X	X	X	X	
	● The effectiveness of pain management, when applicable	X			X	X	
	The organization collects data that measure the performance of each of the following potentially high-risk processes, when provided (EPs 4–12):						
A [0] [1] [2] [NA]	4. Medication management	X	X	X	X	X	X
A [0] [1] [2] [NA]	5. Blood and blood product use	X			X	X	X
A [0] [1] [2] [NA]	6. Restraint use	X	X	X	X	X	
A [0] [1] [2] [NA]	7. Seclusion use		X		X		
A [0] [1] [2] [NA]	8. Behavior management and treatment		X		X	X	
A [0] [1] [2] [NA]	9. Care, treatment, and services provided to high-risk or vulnerable populations as defined by the organization		X				
A [0] [1] [2] [NA]	10. Operative and other invasive procedures				X		

* Joint Commission is moving from the phrase *satisfaction with care, treatment, and services* toward the more inclusive phrase *perception of care, treatment, and services* to better measure the performance of organizations meeting the needs, expectations and concerns of clients. By using this term, the organization will be prompted to assess not only patients' and/or families' satisfaction with care, treatment, or services, but also whether the organization meets their needs and expectations.

† This EP applies to all behavioral health care programs and services **except shelters**.

	AMB	BHC	CAH	HAP	LTC	OBS					
11. Operative and other procedures that place patients at risk	X					X	A	0	1	2	NA
12. Resuscitation and its outcomes				X			A	0	1	2	NA
Relevant information developed from the following activities is integrated into performance improvement initiatives. This occurs in a way consistent with any organization policies or procedures intended to preserve any confidentiality or privilege of information established by applicable law (EPs 13–22):											
13. Risk management		X*	X	X	X	X	B	0	1	2	NA
14. Utilization management	X	X*	X	X	X		B	0	1	2	NA
15. Quality control	X			X	X		B	0	1	2	NA
16. Infection control surveillance and reporting	X	X*	X	X	X	X	B	0	1	2	NA
17. Research, as applicable	X	X	X	X	X		B	0	1	2	NA
18. Autopsies, when performed				X			B	0	1	2	NA
19. Through 22. Not applicable	X	X	X	X	X	X					

Additional Elements of Performance for Medicare-Certified Ambulatory Surgical Centers

	AMB	BHC	CAH	HAP	LTC	OBS					
23. The ambulatory surgery center, with the medical staff's active participation, collects data on an ongoing basis about the medical necessity of procedures.	X						A	0	1	2	NA
24. The ambulatory surgery center, with the medical staff's active participation, collects data on an ongoing basis about the appropriateness of care.	X						A	0	1	2	NA
25. Not applicable	X	X	X	X	X	X					

* This EP applies to all behavioral health care programs and services **except shelters**.

Additional Element of Performance for Opioid Addiction Treatment Programs

B [0 | 1 | 2 | NA]

	AMB	BHC	CAH	HAP	LTC	OBS
26. Outcomes and processes should be measured and monitored such as the following: • Reducing or eliminating the use of illicit opioids, illicit drugs, and the problematic use of illicit drugs • Reducing or eliminating associated criminal activities • Reducing behaviors contributing to the spread of infectious diseases • Improving quality of life by restoration of physical and mental health and functional status		X				

Additional Elements of Performance for Office-Based Surgery

B [0 | 1 | 2 | NA]

B [0 | 1 | 2 | NA]

B [0 | 1 | 2 | NA]

	AMB	BHC	CAH	HAP	LTC	OBS
27. The practice collects data that measures clinical outcomes, including the following: • Adverse clinical events during procedures • Complications following procedures • Complications requiring transfer to an acute care facility • Unplanned, prolonged, or frequent extended stays in recovery • Procedures that once begun are stopped prematurely						X
28. Data that the practice considers for collection to monitor performance include the following: • Care or services provided to high-risk populations • Appropriateness of surgery and anesthesia						X
29. The organization collects and analyzes conversion rate data to monitor organ procurement effectiveness, and when possible, takes steps to improve the conversion rate. **Note:** *Conversion rate is defined as the number of actual organ donors over the number of eligible donors as defined by the organ procurement organization (OPO), expressed as a percentage.*			X	X		

❏ Compliant
❏ Not Compliant

Standard PI.2.20*

Undesirable patterns or trends in performance are analyzed.

Elements of Performance for PI.2.20

	AMB	BHC	CAH	HAP	LTC	OBS
B 1. Analysis is performed when data comparisons indicate that levels of performance, patterns, or trends vary substantially from those expected.	X	X	X	X	X	X

---

* This standard, its rationale, and its EPs apply to all behavioral health care programs and services **except shelters**.

	AMB	BHC	CAH	HAP	LTC	OBS		
2. Analysis occurs for those topics chosen by leaders as performance improvement priorities.	X	X	X	X	X	X	**B**	0 1 2 NA
3. Analysis is performed when undesirable variation occurs which changes priorities.	X	X	X	X	X		**B**	0 1 2 NA
An analysis is performed for the following (EPs 4–9):								
4. All confirmed transfusion reactions, if applicable to the organization	X		X	X	X		**A**	0 1 2 NA
5. All serious adverse drug events, if applicable and as defined by the organization	X	X	X	X	X	X	**A**	0 1 2 NA
6. All significant medication errors, if applicable and as defined by the organization	X	X	X	X	X	X	**A**	0 1 2 NA
7. All major discrepancies between preoperative and postoperative (including pathologic) diagnoses	X		X	X		X	**A**	0 1 2 NA
8. Adverse events or patterns of adverse events during moderate or deep sedation and anesthesia use	X		X	X		X	**A**	0 1 2 NA
9. Hazardous conditions*	X	X	X	X	X		**A**	0 1 2 NA
10. Staffing effectiveness issues				X	X		**A**	0 1 2 NA
11. Not applicable	X	X	X	X	X	X		
An analysis is performed for the following: 12. Errors and omissions in patient assessment for surgery and anesthesia resulting in significant adverse clinical events						X	**A**	0 1 2 NA
13. An analysis is performed for the following: ORYX core measure data that, over three or more consecutive quarters for the same measure, identify the organization as a negative outlier.				X			**A**	0 1 2 NA

* **(AHC only)** Any set of circumstances, defined by the organization, (exclusive of the disease or condition for which the individual is being treated), which significantly increases the likelihood of a serious adverse outcome.

❏ Compliant
❏ Not Compliant

Standard PI.2.30*

Processes for identifying and managing sentinel events are defined and implemented.

Rationale for PI.2.30

	AMB	BHC	CAH	HAP	LTC	OBS
Identifying, reporting, analyzing, and managing sentinel events can help the organization to prevent such incidents. Leaders define and implement such a program as part of the process to measure, assess, and improve the organization's performance.	X	X	X	X	X	

Elements of Performance for PI.2.30

Processes for identifying and managing sentinel events include the following (EPs 1–4):

		AMB	BHC	CAH	HAP	LTC	OBS
A [0][1][2][NA]	1. Defining "sentinel event" and communicating this definition throughout the organization. (At a minimum, the organization's definition includes those events subject to review under the Joint Commission's Sentinel Event Policy as published in the accreditation manuals and may include any process variation which does not affect the outcome or result in an adverse event, but for which a recurrence carries significant chance of a serious adverse outcome, often referred to as a "near miss.")	X	X	X	X	X	X
A [0][1][2][NA]	2. Reporting sentinel events through established channels in the organization and, as appropriate, to external agencies in accordance with law and regulation.	X	X	X	X	X	X
B [0][1][2][NA]	3. Conducting thorough and credible root cause analyses that focus on process and system factors.	X	X	X	X	X	X
B [0][1][2][NA]	4. Creating, documenting, and implementing a risk-reduction strategy and action plan that includes measuring the effectiveness of process and system improvements to reduce risk.	X	X	X	X	X	X
B [0][1][2][NA]	5. The processes are implemented.	X	X	X	X	X	X

---

* This standard, its rationale, and its EPs apply to all behavioral health care programs and services **except shelters**.

Standard PI.3.20*

An ongoing, proactive program for identifying and reducing unanticipated adverse events and safety risks to patients is defined and implemented.

Rationale for PI.3.20

	AMB	BHC	CAH	HAP	LTC	OBS
Organizations should proactively seek to identify and reduce risks to the safety of patients. Such initiatives have the obvious advantage of *preventing* adverse events rather than simply *reacting* when they occur. This approach also avoids the barriers to understanding created by hindsight bias and the fear of disclosure, embarrassment, blame, and punishment that can happen after an event.	X	X	X	X	X	X

Elements of Performance for PI.3.20

The following proactive activities to reduce risks to patients are conducted (EPs 1–9):

	AMB	BHC	CAH	HAP	LTC	OBS					
1. Selecting a high-risk process† to be analyzed (at least one high-risk process is chosen annually‡—the choice should be based in part on information published periodically by the Joint Commission about the most frequent sentinel events and risks)	X	X	X	X	X	X	A	0	1	2	NA
2. Describing the chosen process (for example, through the use of a flowchart)	X	X	X	X	X	X	B	0	1	2	NA
3. Identifying the ways in which the process could break down§ or fail to perform its desired function	X	X	X	X	X	X	B	0	1	2	NA
4. Identifying the possible effects that a breakdown or failure of the process could have on patients and the seriousness of the possible effects	X	X	X	X	X	X	B	0	1	2	NA
5. Prioritizing the potential process breakdowns or failures	X	X	X	X	X	X	B	0	1	2	NA

* This standard, its rationale, and its EPs apply to all behavioral health care programs and services **except shelters**.

† **High-risk process** A process that if not planned and/or implemented correctly, has a significant potential for impacting the safety of the patient.

‡ **[AHC & BHC ONLY]** On rare occasions, the organization may determine that it has no high-risk processes to be analyzed due to the nature of the care, treatment, and services provided. If this situation occurs, the organization must document on an annual basis that it has determined there are no high-risk processes as well as the reasons for the determination. Additionally, there may be rare occasions when the organization has a limited number of high-risk processes due to the nature of the care, treatment, and services provided. In those instances, the organization can re analyze a high-risk processes, provided that all identified high-risk processes related to the care, treatment, and services provided have been reviewed.

§ The ways in which processes could break down or fail to perform its desired function are many times referred to as "the failure modes".

B [0 | 1 | 2 | NA]

B [0 | 1 | 2 | NA]

B [0 | 1 | 2 | NA]

B [0 | 1 | 2 | NA]

	AMB	BHC	CAH	HAP	LTC	OBS
6. Determining why the prioritized breakdowns or failures could occur, which may include performing a hypothetical root cause analysis	X	X	X	X	X	X
7. Redesigning the process and/or underlying systems to minimize the risk of the effects on patients	X	X	X	X	X	X
8. Testing and implementing the redesigned process	X	X	X	X	X	X
9. Monitoring the effectiveness of the redesigned process	X	X	X	X	X	X

Leadership

❏ Compliant
❏ Not Compliant

Standard LD.4.20*

New or modified services or processes are designed well.

Elements of Performance for LD.4.20

The design of new or modified services or processes incorporates the following (EPs 1–6):

B [0 | 1 | 2 | NA]

B [0 | 1 | 2 | NA]

B [0 | 1 | 2 | NA]

B [0 | 1 | 2 | NA]

B [0 | 1 | 2 | NA]

B [0 | 1 | 2 | NA]

B [0 | 1 | 2 | NA]

	AMB	BHC	CAH	HAP	LTC	OBS
1. The needs and expectations of patients, staff, and others	X	X	X	X	X	
2. The results of performance improvement activities, when available	X	X	X	X	X	
3. Information about potential risks to patients, when available	X	X	X	X	X	
4. Current knowledge, when available and relevant (for example, practice guidelines, successful practices, information from relevant literature, and clinical standards)	X	X	X	X	X	
5. Information about sentinel events, when available and relevant	X	X	X	X	X	
6. Testing and analysis to determine whether the proposed design or redesign is an improvement	X	X	X	X	X	X
7. The leaders collaborate with staff and appropriate stakeholders to design services.	X	X	X	X	X	

* This standard, its rationale, and its EPs apply to all behavioral health care programs and services **except shelters**.

Standard LD.4.40*

The leaders ensure that an integrated patient safety program is implemented throughout the organization.

Rationale for LD.4.40

	AMB	BHC	CAH	HAP	LTC	OBS
The leaders should work to foster a safe environment throughout the organization by integrating safety priorities into all relevant organization processes, functions, and services. In pursuit of this effort, a patient safety program can work to improve safety by reducing the risk of system or process failures. As part of its responsibility to communicate objectives and coordinate efforts to integrate patient care and support services throughout the organization and with contracted services, leadership takes the lead in developing, implementing, and overseeing a patient safety program. The standard does not require the creation of new structures or "offices" in the organization; rather, the standard emphasizes the need to integrate all patient-safety activities, both existing and newly created, with the organization's leadership identified as accountable for this integration.	X	X	X	X	X	X

Elements of Performance for LD.4.40

The patient safety program includes the following (EPs 1–8):

	AMB	BHC	CAH	HAP	LTC	OBS					
1. One or more qualified individuals or an interdisciplinary group assigned to manage the organizationwide safety program	X	X	X	X	X	X	**A**	0	1	2	NA
2. Definition of the scope of the program's oversight, typically ranging from no-harm, frequently occurring "slips" to sentinel events with serious adverse outcomes	X	X	X	X	X	X	**B**	0	1	2	NA
3. Integration into and participation of all components of the organization into the organizationwide program	X	X	X	X	X	X	**B**	0	1	2	NA
4. Procedures for immediately responding to system or process failures, including care, treatment, and services for the affected individual(s), containing risk to others, and preserving factual information for subsequent analysis	X	X	X	X	X	X	**B**	0	1	2	NA
5. Clear systems for internal and external reporting of information about system or process failures	X	X	X	X	X	X	**B**	0	1	2	NA
6. Defined responses to various types of unanticipated adverse events and processes for conducting proactive risk assessment/ risk reduction activities	X	X	X	X	X	X	**B**	0	1	2	NA

---

* This standard, its rationale, and its EPs apply to all behavioral health care programs and services **except shelters**.

B | 0 | 1 | 2 | NA |

A | 0 | 1 | 2 | NA |

	AMB	BHC	CAH	HAP	LTC	OBS
7. Defined support systems* for staff members who have been involved in a sentinel event	X	X	X	X	X	X
8. Reports, at least annually, to the organization's governance or authority on system or process failures and actions taken to improve safety, both proactively and in response to actual occurrences	X	X	X	X	X	X

Management of the Environment of Care

❑ Compliant
❑ Not Compliant

Standard EC.9.10†

The organization monitors conditions in the environment.

Elements of Performance for EC.9.10

B | 0 | 1 | 2 | NA |

	AHC	BHC	CAH	HAP	LTC	OBS
1. The organization establishes and implements process(es) for reporting and investigating the following:‡	X	X§	X	X	X	
• Injuries to patients or others coming to the organization's facilities, as well as incidents of property damage	X	X	X	X	X	
• Occupational illnesses and injuries to staff	X	X	X	X	X	
• Security incidents involving patients, staff, or others coming to the organization's facilities or property	X	X	X	X	X	
• Hazardous materials and waste spills, exposures, and other related incidents	X	X	X	X	X	
• Fire-safety management problems, deficiencies, and failures	X	X	X	X	X	
• Equipment-management problems, failures, and user errors	X	X	X	X	X	
• Utility systems management problems, failures, or user errors	X	X	X	X	X	

---

* Support systems provide individuals with additional help and support as well as additional resources through the human resources function or an employee assistance program. Support systems recognize that conscientious health care workers who are involved in sentinel events are themselves victims of the event and require support. Support systems also focus on the process rather than blaming the involved individuals.

† This standard and its EPs are **not applicable** to office-based surgery practices.

‡ Organizations have the flexibility to develop a single reporting method that addresses one or more of the items listed.

§ This EP applies to all behavioral health care programs and services **except case management, corrections, family preservation/wrap-around, foster care, therapeutic foster care, in-home,** and **online**.

	AHC	BHC	CAH	HAP	LTC	OBS					
2. The organization's leaders assign a person(s) (hereafter referred to as the "assigned person[s]") to monitor and respond to conditions in the organization's environment. The assigned individual performs the following tasks:	X	X*		X	X		**B**	0	1	2	NA
• Coordinates the ongoing, organizationwide collection of information about deficiencies and opportunities for improvement in the environment of care	X	X		X	X						
• Coordinates the ongoing collection and dissemination of other sources of information, such as published hazard notices or recall reports	X	X		X	X						
• Coordinates the preparation of summaries of deficiencies, problems, failures, and user errors related to managing the environment of care†	X	X		X	X						
• Coordinates the preparation of summaries on findings, recommendations, actions taken, and results of performance improvement (PI) activities	X	X		X	X						
• Participates in hazard surveillance and incident reporting	X	X		X	X						
• Participates in developing safety policies and procedures	X	X		X	X						
3. The organization establishes and implements a process(es) for ongoing monitoring of performance regarding actual or potential risk(s) in each of the environment of care management plans.‡	X	X§		X	X		**B**	0	1	2	NA
4. Each of the environment of care management plans is evaluated at least annually.	X	X‖		X	X		**A**	0	1	2	NA

---

* This EP applies to all behavioral health care programs and services **except case management, corrections, family preservation/wrap-around, foster care, therapeutic foster care, in-home,** and **online.**

† **Notes:** *Incidents involving patients may be reported to appropriate staff such as staff in quality assessment, improvement, or other functions. However, at least a summary of incidents is shared with the person designated to coordinate safety management activities (see standard EC.1.10 in the accreditation manual). Review of incident reports often requires that various legal processes be followed to preserve confidentiality. Opportunities to improve care, treatment, and services or to prevent future similar incidents are not lost as a result of the legal process followed.*

‡ The environment of care plans are for managing safety, security, hazardous materials and waste, emergency management, fire safety, (**AHC, HAP, LTC:** medical equipment), and utilities.

§ This EP applies to all behavioral health care programs and services **except case management, corrections, family preservation/wrap-around, foster care, therapeutic foster care, in-home,** and **online.**

‖ This EP applies to all behavioral health care programs and services **except case management, corrections, family preservation/wrap-around, foster care, therapeutic foster care, in-home,** and **online.**

Scoring Grid

0 Insufficient compliance
1 Partial compliance
2 Satisfactory compliance
NA Not applicable

B [0 | 1 | 2 | NA]

		AMB	BHC	CAH	HAP	LTC	OBS
5.	The objectives, scope, performance, and effectiveness of each of the environment of care management plans are evaluated at least annually.	X	X*		X	X	
6.	Not applicable	X	X	X	X	X	
7.	Not applicable	X	X	X	X	X	
8.	Not applicable	X	X	X	X	X	
9.	Not applicable	X	X	X	X	X	
10.	Environmental safety monitoring and response activities are communicated to the patient safety program required in the "Leadership" chapter of the accreditation manuals.	X	X†		X	X	

B [0 | 1 | 2 | NA] (row 10)

❑ Compliant
❑ Not Compliant

Standard EC.9.20‡

The organization analyzes identified environment issues and develops recommendations for resolving them.

Elements of Performance for EC.9.20

B [0 | 1 | 2 | NA]

C [0 | 1 | 2 | NA]

B [0 | 1 | 2 | NA]

		AMB	BHC	CAH	HAP	LTC	OBS
1.	The organization establishes an ongoing process for resolving environment of care issues that involves representatives from clinical, administrative, and support services.	X	X§		X	X	
2.	A multidisciplinary improvement team meets at least bimonthly to address environment of care issues.‖ 				X	X	
3.	The organization analyzes environment of care issues in a timely manner.	X	X**		X	X	

---

* This EP applies to all behavioral health care programs and services **except case management, corrections, family preservation/wrap-around, foster care, therapeutic foster care, in-home,** and **online.**

† This EP applies to all behavioral health care programs and services **except case management, corrections, family preservation/wrap-around, foster care, therapeutic foster care, in-home,** and **online.**

‡ This standard and its EPs are **not applicable** to critical access hospitals and office-based surgery practices.

§ This EP applies to all behavioral health care programs and services **except case management, corrections, family preservation/wrap-around, foster care, therapeutic foster care, in-home,** and **online.**

‖ **Note:** *Meetings held less frequently than bimonthly are acceptable when supported by current organization experience and the multidisciplinary improvement team's approval. Ongoing justification of meeting frequency depends on a satisfactory annual evaluation of performance as required by EC.9.10.*

** This EP applies to all behavioral health care programs and services **except case management, corrections, family preservation/wrap-around, foster care, therapeutic foster care, in-home,** and **online.**

	AMB	BHC	CAH	HAP	LTC	OBS					
4. Recommendations are developed and approved as appropriate.	X	X*		X	X		**B**	0	1	2	NA
5. Appropriate staff establishes measurement guidelines.	X	X*		X			**B**	0	1	2	NA
6. Environment of care issues are communicated to the organization's leaders and person(s) responsible for PI activities.	X	X*		X	X		**B**	0	1	2	NA
7. Not applicable	X	X		X	X						
8. A recommendation for one or more PI activities is communicated at least annually to the organization's leaders based on the ongoing performance monitoring of the environment of care management plans.	X	X*		X	X		**A**	0	1	2	NA
9. Recommendations for resolving environmental safety issues are communicated, when appropriate, to those responsible for managing the individual safety program required in the "Leadership" chapter of the accreditation manuals.	X	X*		X	X		**B**	0	1	2	NA

Standard EC.9.30[†]

The organization improves the environment.

❏ Compliant
❏ Not Compliant

Elements of Performance for EC.9.30

	AMB	BHC	CAH	HAP	LTC	OBS					
1. Appropriate staff participates in implementing recommendations.	X	X*		X	X		**B**	0	1	2	NA
2. Appropriate staff monitors the effectiveness of the recommendation's implementation.	X	X*		X	X		**B**	0	1	2	NA
3. Monitoring results are reported through appropriate channels, including the organization's leaders.	X	X*		X							

---

[*] This EP applies to all behavioral health care programs and services **except case management, corrections, family preservation/wrap-around, foster care, therapeutic foster care, in-home,** and **online**.

[†] This standard and its EPs are **not applicable** to critical access hospitals and office-based surgery practices.

B [0 | 1 | 2 | NA]

B [0 | 1 | 2 | NA]

		AMB	BHC	CAH	HAP	LTC	OBS
4.	Monitoring results are reported to the multidisciplinary improvement team responsible for resolving environment of care issues.				X	X	
5.	Results of monitoring are reported (when appropriate) to those responsible for managing the patient safety program required in the "Leadership" chapter of the accreditation manuals.	X	X*		X	X	

Management of Human Resources

❑ Compliant
❑ Not Compliant

Standard HR.2.30†

Ongoing education, including in-services, training, and other activities, maintains and improves competence.

Rationale for HR.2.30

	AMB	BHC	CAH	HAP	LTC	OBS
When developing recruitment, retention, development, and continuing education processes for all staff, the leaders consider the following factors: • The practice's goals and values • The case mix of patients and the degree and complexity of care they require • Technology used in patient care, treatment, and services • Identified learning needs						X

Elements of Performance for HR.2.30

The following occurs for staff, students, and volunteers† who work in the same capacity as staff providing care, treatment, and services (EPs 1–8):

B [0 | 1 | 2 | NA]

C [0 | 1 | 2 | NA]

C [0 | 1 | 2 | NA]

		AMB	BHC	CAH	HAP	LTC	OBS
1.	Training occurs when job responsibilities or duties change	X	X	X	X	X	X
2.	Participation in ongoing in-services, training, or other activities occurs to increase staff, student, or volunteer knowledge of work-related issues Ⓜ	X	X	X	X	X	X
3.	Ongoing in-services and other education and training are appropriate to the needs of the population(s) served and comply with law and regulation Ⓜ	X	X	X	X	X	

* This EP applies to all behavioral health care programs and services **except case management, corrections, family preservation/wrap-around, foster care, therapeutic foster care, in-home,** and **online**.

† This standard, its rationale, and its EPs apply to all behavioral health care programs and services **except shelters**.

‡ "Volunteers" **does not apply** to office-based surgery practices.

	AMB	BHC	CAH	HAP	LTC	OBS					
4. Ongoing in-services, training, or other activities emphasize specific job-related aspects of safety and infection prevention and control ⓜ	X	X	X	X	X		**C**	0	1	2	NA
5. Ongoing in-services, training, or other education incorporate methods of team training, when appropriate ⓜ	X	X	X	X	X		**C**	0	1	2	NA
6. Ongoing in-services, training, or other education reinforce the need and ways to report unanticipated adverse events ⓜ		X	X	X	X	X	**C**	0	1	2	NA
7. Ongoing in-services or other education is offered in response to learning needs identified through performance improvement findings and other data analysis (that is, data from staff surveys, performance evaluations, or other needs assessments) ⓜ	X	X	X	X	X		**C**	0	1	2	NA
8. Ongoing education is documented ⓜ		X	X	X	X	X		**C**	0	1	2	NA
9. Not applicable		X	X	X	X	X	X					
10. Staff members are educated, as appropriate to their responsibilities, about psychotropic medications including, the following: ● The need for a medication in relation to the resident's documented diagnosis and condition ● The potential for drug-drug and drug-food interactions ● Adverse reactions to psychotropic medications ● The use of a medication for an appropriate duration ● The optimal dose ● Frequent monitoring of the medication's effectiveness ● Nonmedication interventions and alternatives developed through the interdisciplinary team assessment ● Reduction and discontinuation of a medication					X		**B**	0	1	2	NA
11. Supervision and consultation are available to direct care staff to maintain and enhance their knowledge, skills, and attitudes in providing care, treatment, and services.		X					**B**	0	1	2	NA

Additional Elements of Performance for Opioid Addiction Treatment Programs

	AMB	BHC	CAH	HAP	LTC	OBS					
12. Staff is trained to respond to medical emergencies. ⓜ		X					**C**	0	1	2	NA
13. Staff is trained in the specific characteristics and needs of women participating in the program. ⓜ		X					**C**	0	1	2	NA
14. Individual annual training programs are implemented.		X					**B**	0	1	2	NA
15. Staff has resources for problem solving and troubleshooting.		X					**B**	0	1	2	NA
16. Records are maintained for staff training events. ⓜ		X					**C**	0	1	2	NA

Scoring Grid

0	Insufficient compliance
1	Partial compliance
2	Satisfactory compliance
NA	Not applicable

Management of Information

Information Management Planning

❏ Compliant
❏ Not Compliant

Standard IM.1.10*,†

The organization plans and designs information management processes to meet internal and external information needs.

Rationale for IM.1.10

	AMB	BHC	CAH	HAP	LTC	OBS
Organizations vary in size, complexity, governance, structure, decision-making processes, and resources. Information management systems and processes vary accordingly. Only by first identifying the information needs can one then evaluate the extent to which they are planned for, and at what performance level the needs are being met. Planning for the management of information does not require a formal written information plan, but does require evidence of a planned approach that identifies the organization's information needs and supports its goals and objectives.	X	X	X	X	X	X

Elements of Performance for IM.1.10

	AMB	BHC	CAH	HAP	LTC	OBS
1. The organization bases its information management processes on an assessment of internal and external information needs.	X	X	X	X	X	
• The assessment identifies the flow of information throughout an organization, including information storage and feedback mechanisms.	X	X	X	X	X	
• The assessment identifies the data and information needed: within and among departments, services, or programs; within and among the staff, the administration, and the governance for supporting relationships with outside services and contractors; with licensing, accrediting, and regulatory bodies; with purchasers, payers, and employers; for supporting informational needs between the organization and the patients; and for participating in research and databases.	X	X	X	X	X	

B | 0 | 1 | 2 | NA

---

* This standard, its rationale, and its EPs are **not applicable** to office-based surgery practices.

† This standard, its rationale, and its EPs apply to all behavioral health care programs and services.

	AMB	BHC	CAH	HAP	LTC	OBS
2. To guide development of processes for managing information used internally and externally, the organization assesses its information management needs based on the following: ● Its mission ● Its goals ● Its services ● Personnel ● Patient safety considerations ● Quality of care, treatment, and services ● Mode(s) of service delivery ● Resources ● Access to affordable technology ● Identification of barriers to effective communication among caregivers	X	X	X	X	X	
3. The organization bases its management, staffing, and material resource allocations for information management on the scope and complexity of care, treatment, and services provided.	X	X		X	X	
4. Identified staff participates in assessment, selection, integration, and use of information management systems for clinical/service and organization information.	X	X	X	X	X	
5. The organization has an ongoing process to assess the needs of the organization, departments, and individuals for knowledge-based information.	X	X	X	X	X	
6. The organization uses the assessment for knowledge-based information and as a basis for planning.	X	X		X	X	
7. The critical access hospital has an agreement with at least one hospital for the development and use of communications systems, including the hospital's system for the electronic sharing of patient data, and telemetry and medical records, if the hospital has such a system in operation.			X			

Scoring column (for each row 2–7):

B 0 1 2 NA

Standard IM.3.10[*,†]

The organization has processes in place to effectively manage information, including the capturing, reporting, processing, storing, retrieving, disseminating, and displaying of clinical/service and nonclinical data and information.

Rationale for IM.3.10

	AMB	BHC	CAH	HAP	LTC	OBS
Records resulting from data capture and report generation[†] are used for communication and continuity of the patient's care or financial and business operations over time. Records are also used for other purposes, including litigation and risk management activities, reimbursement, and statistics. Improved data capture and report generation systems enhance the value of the records. Potential benefits include improved patient care quality and safety, improved efficiency, effectiveness, and reduced costs in patient care, and financial and business operations. To maximize the benefits of data capture and report generation, these processes exhibit the following characteristics: unique ID, accuracy, completeness, timeliness[§], interoperability[‖], retrievability[**], authentication and accountability[††], auditability, confidentiality, and security. The processing, storage, and retrieval functions are integral to electronic, computerized, and paper-based information systems in organizations. Important considerations for these functions include data elements, data accuracy, data confidentiality, data security, data integrity, permanence of storage (the time a medium can safely store information), ease of retrievability, aggregation of information, interoperability, clinical/service practice considerations, performance improvement, and decision support processing. A goal for information storage is to be linked or centrally organized and accessible. This could include the organization having an index identifying where the information is stored and how to access it; or, as the organization moves to electronic systems, the organization creates all information systems to be interoperable within the enterprise. As more organizations automate various processes and activities, it is important to share critical data among systems. As challenges of interoperability have arisen, standards organizations have stepped in to develop industry standards. It is important that the organization is aware of the standards development organizations and their recommendations.	X	X	X	X	X	

---

[*] This standard, its rationale, and its EPs are **not applicable** to office-based surgery practices.

[†] This standard, its rationale, and its EPs apply to all behavioral health care programs and services **except shelters**.

[‡] **Report generation** The process of analyzing, organizing, and presenting recorded information for authentication and inclusion in the patient's health care record or in financial or business records.

[§] **Timeliness** The time between the occurrence of an event and the availability of data about the event. Timeliness is related to the use of the data.

[‖] **Interoperability** Enables authorized users to capture, share, and report information from any system, whether paper-or electronic-based.

[**] **Retrievability** The capability of efficiently finding relevant information.

[††] **Accountability** All information is attributable to its source (person or device).

	AMB	BHC	CAH	HAP	LTC	OBS
Internally and externally generated data and information are accurately disseminated to users. Access to accurate information is required to deliver, improve, analyze, and advance patient care and the systems that support health care delivery. Information may be accessed and disseminated through electronic information systems or paper-based records and reports. The use of information should be considered in developing forms, screen displays, and standard or ad hoc reports.						

Elements of Performance for IM.3.10

	AMB	BHC	CAH	HAP	LTC	OBS		
1. Information technology industry standards or organization policies are used and address the following: • Uniform data definitions • Data capture • Data display • Data transmission	X	X	X	X	X		B	0 1 2 NA
2. Standardize a list of abbreviations, acronyms, and symbols that are not to be used throughout the organization. Ⓜ	X	X	X	X	X			
3. Minimum data sets, terminology, definitions, classifications, vocabulary, and nomenclature, including abbreviations, acronyms, and symbols, are standardized throughout the organization.	X	X	X	X	X		B	0 1 2 NA
4. Quality control systems are used to monitor data content and collection activities. • The method used provides for timely and economical data collection with the degree of accuracy, completeness, and discrimination necessary for their intended use. • The method used minimizes bias in the data and regularly assesses the data's reliability, validity, and accuracy. • Those responsible for collecting and reviewing the data are accountable for information accuracy and completeness.	X	X	X	X	X		B	0 1 2 NA
5. Storage and retrieval systems are designed to support organization needs for clinical/service and organization-specific information. • Storage and retrieval systems are designed to balance the ability to retrieve data and information with the intended use for the data and information. • Storage and retrieval systems are designed to balance security and confidentiality issues with accessibility. • Systems for paper and electronic records are designed to reduce disruption or inaccessibility during such times as diminished staffing and scheduled and unscheduled downtimes of electronic information systems.	X	X	X	X	X		B	0 1 2 NA
6. Data and information are retained for sufficient time to comply with law and regulation.	X	X	X	X	X		B	0 1 2 NA

B | 0 | 1 | 2 | NA

B | 0 | 1 | 2 | NA

B | 0 | 1 | 2 | NA

B | 0 | 1 | 2 | NA

	AMB	BHC	CAH	HAP	LTC	OBS
7. Knowledgeable staff and tools are available for collecting, retrieving, and analyzing data and their transformation into information.	X	X	X	X	X	
8. Data are organized and transformed into information in formats useful to decision makers.	X	X		X	X	
9. Dissemination of data and information is timely* and accurate.	X	X		X	X	
10. Data and information are disseminated in standard formats and methods to meet user needs and provide for easy retrievability and interpretation.	X	X	X	X	X	

Additional Element of Performance for Opioid Addiction Treatment Programs

B | 0 | 1 | 2 | NA

	AMB	BHC	CAH	HAP	LTC	OBS
12. Programs should develop and implement procedures to avoid duplication of information gathering without compromising objectives of multiple agencies. Ⓜ		X				

Information-Based Decision Making

❏ Compliant
❏ Not Compliant

Standard IM.4.10†,‡

The information management system provides information for use in decision making.

Rationale for IM.4.10

	AMB	BHC	CAH	HAP	LTC	OBS
Information management supports timely and effective decision making at all organization levels. The information management processes support managerial and operational decisions, performance improvement activities, and patient care, treatment, and service decisions. Clinical and strategic decision making depends on information from multiple sources, including the patient record, knowledge-based information, comparative data/information, and aggregate data/information.	X	X	X	X	X	

---

* **Timely** Defined by organization policy and based on the intended use of the information.

† This standard, its rationale, and its EPs are **not applicable** to office-based surgery practices.

‡ This standard, its rationale, and its EPs apply to all behavioral health care programs and services **except shelters**.

Elements of Performance for IM.4.10

To support clinical decision making, information found in the patient record must include the following:

	AMB	BHC	CAH	HAP	LTC	OBS
1. The organization has the ability to collect and aggregate data and information to support care, treatment, and service delivery and operations, including the following: • Individual care, treatment, and services and care, treatment, and service delivery • Decision making • Management and operations • Analysis of trends • Performance comparisons over time throughout the organization and with other organizations • Performance improvement • Infection control • Patient safety	X	X		X	X	
2. To support clinical decision making, information found in the patient record is the following: • Readily accessible • Accurate • Complete • Organized for retrieval of data • Timely	X	X		X	X	
3. Comparative performance data and information are used for decision making, when available.	X	X		X	X	

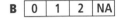

B   0   1   2   NA

❏ Compliant
❏ Not Compliant

Knowledge-Based Information

Standard IM.5.10*,†

Knowledge-based information resources are readily available, current, and authoritative.

Rationale for IM.5.10

	AMB	BHC	CAH	HAP	LTC	OBS
Organization practitioners and staff have access to knowledge-based‡ information to do the following: ● Acquire and maintain the knowledge and skills needed to maintain and improve competence ● Assist with clinical/service and management decision making ● Provide appropriate information and education to patients and families ● Support performance improvement and patient safety activities ● Support the institution's educational and research needs	X	X	X	X	X	

Elements of Performance for IM.5.10

		AMB	BHC	CAH	HAP	LTC	OBS
A	1. Library services are provided by cooperative or contractual arrangements with other institutions, if not available on site.			X	X		
B	2. The organization provides access to knowledge-based‡§ information resources needed by staff in any of the following formats: print, electronic, internet, audio.	X	X	X	X	X	
B	3. Knowledge-based information resources are available to clinical/service staff, through electronic means, after-hours access to an in-house collection, or other methods.	X	X	X	X	X	
B	4. The organization has a process for providing access to knowledge-based information resources when electronic systems are unavailable.	X	X		X	X	

Scoring boxes (left margin):
A [0 | 1 | 2 | NA]
B [0 | 1 | 2 | NA]
B [0 | 1 | 2 | NA]
B [0 | 1 | 2 | NA]

---

* This standard, its rationale, and its EPs are **not applicable** to office-based surgery practices.

† This standard, its rationale, and its EPs apply to all behavioral health care programs and services **except shelters**.

‡ **Knowledge-based information** A collection of stored facts, models, and information that can be used for designing and redesigning processes and for problem solving. In the context of the accreditation manuals, knowledge-based information is found in the clinical, scientific, and management literature.

§ Examples of knowledge-based information resources include current texts; periodicals; indexes; abstracts; reports; documents; databases; directories; discussion lists; successful practices; equipment and maintenance user manuals; standards; protocols; practice guidelines; clinical trials, and other resources.

Matrix 2: Patient Safety Standards, Rationales, Elements of Performance, and Scoring Information for Home Care Organizations

The patient safety standards, rationales, elements of performance, and scoring information for home care organizations are included in a separate matrix because of the unique applicability grids that accompany each standard and EP. The grids indicate the applicability of all the home care safety standards and EPs. An X in a home care service column indicates to which of the following 10 home care services each standard and EP applies:[*]

HH	Home health
PC/SS	Personal care and support services
HSP	Hospice
Pharm Disp	Pharmacy dispensing services
C/C Pharm	Clinical or consultant pharmacist services
LTC Pharm	Long term care pharmacy services
Amb Infusion	Freestanding (non-physician-based) ambulatory infusion services
HME	Home medical equipment
CRS	Clinical respiratory services
RT	Rehabilitation technology services

See pages 71–73 for directions on how to score the standards and elements of performance.

Standard RI.2.90

Patients and, when appropriate, their families are informed about the outcomes of care, treatment, and services that have been provided, including unanticipated outcomes.

❏ Compliant
❏ Not Compliant

The standard above applies to the following services:

	HH	PC/SS	HSP	Pharm Disp	C/C Pharm	LTC Pharm	Amb Infusion	HME	CRS	RT
RI.2.90	X	X	X	X	X	X	X	X	X	X

Rationale for RI.2.90

Patients may experience anticipated outcomes of care such as side effects. Sometimes, outcomes may not have been anticipated (e.g., malfunctioning infusion pumps, problems with a bili light). Often patients are made aware of these events when they happen. Whatever the event and whenever it occurs, the patient must be informed.

---

[*]For definitions of each home care service, please see the Glossary in the *2006–2007 Comprehensive Accreditation Manual for Home Care.*

Elements of Performance for RI.2.90

The elements of performance below apply to the following services:

	HH	PC/SS	HSP	Pharm Disp	C/C Pharm	LTC Pharm	Amb Infusion	HME	CRS	RT
EP 1	X	X	X	X	X	X	X	X	X	X
EP 2	X	X	X	X	X	X	X	X	X	X
EP 3	X	X	X	X	X	X	X	X	X	X

C [0 | 1 | 2 | NA]

🅜 1. At a minimum, the patient (and when appropriate, his or her family) is informed about the following: Outcomes of care, treatment, and services that have been provided that the patient (or family) must be knowledgeable about to participate in current and future decisions affecting the patient's care, treatment, and services.

C [0 | 1 | 2 | NA]

🅜 2. At a minimum, the patient (and when appropriate, his or her family) is informed about the following: Unanticipated outcomes of care, treatment, and services that relate to sentinel events considered reviewable* by the Joint Commission.

C [0 | 1 | 2 | NA]

🅜 3. The leader of the organization or his or her designee informs the patient (and when appropriate, his or her family) about those unanticipated outcomes of care, treatment, and services related to sentinel events, when the patient is not already aware of the occurrence, or further discussion is needed (*see* element of performance 2 above).[†]

❏ Compliant
❏ Not Compliant

Standard PI.1.10

The organization collects data to monitor its performance.

The standard above applies to the following services:

	HH	PC/SS	HSP	Pharm Disp	C/C Pharm	LTC Pharm	Amb Infusion	HME	CRS	RT
PI.1.10	X	X	X	X	X	X	X	X	X	X

Rationale for PI.1.10

Data help determine performance improvement priorities. The data collected for high-priority areas and required areas are used to monitor the stability of existing processes, identify opportunities for improvement, identify changes that lead to improvement, or sustain improvement. Data collection helps identify specific areas that require further study. These areas are determined by considering the information provided by the data about process stability, risks, and sentinel events, as well as priorities set by the leaders. Data may come from internal sources such as staff or external sources such as patients, referral sources, and so on. In addition, the organization identifies those areas needing improvement and identifies desired changes. Performance measures are used to determine whether the changes result in desired outcomes. The organization identifies the frequency and detail of data collection.

Note: *The organization also collects scorable data on the following areas:*
● *Evaluation and improvement of conditions in the environment (see the "Environmental Safety and Equipment Management" chapter)*

---

* *See* the "Sentinel Events" chapter of the *2006–2007 CAMHC* for a definition of reviewable sentinel events.

† In settings where there is no licensed independent practitioner, the staff member responsible for the care of the patient is responsible for sharing information about such outcomes.

Elements of Performance for PI.1.10

The elements of performance below apply to the following services:

	HH	PC/SS	HSP	Pharm Disp	C/C Pharm	LTC Pharm	Amb Infusion	HME	CRS	RT
EP 1	X	X	X	X	X	X	X	X	X	X
EP 2	X	X	X	X	X	X	X	X	X	X
EP 3	X	X	X	X	X	X	X	X	X	X
EP 4	X[3]		X	X	X	X	X		X	X
EP 5	X		X				X			
EP 13	X	X	X	X	X	X	X	X	X	X
EP 14	X	X	X	X	X	X	X	X	X	X
EP 15	X	X	X	X	X	X	X	X	X	X
EP 16	X	X	X	X	X	X	X	X	X	X
EP 17	X	X	X	X	X	X	X	X	X	X
EP 25			X[3]							

[3] Applies to Medicare-certified home health agencies only

1. The organization collects data for priorities identified by leaders (*see* standard LD.4.50).

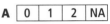

2. The organization considers collecting data in the following areas:
    - Staff opinions and needs
    - Staff perceptions of risks to individuals and suggestions for improving patient safety
    - Staff willingness to report unanticipated adverse events
    - Conditions in the organization or individual environment related to care, treatment, and services provided

3. The organization collects data on the perceptions of care, treatment, and services* of patients including the following:
    - Their specific needs and expectations
    - How well the organization meets these needs and expectations
    - How the organization can improve patient safety
    - The effectiveness of pain management, when applicable

B 0 1 2 NA

The organization collects data that measure the performance of each of the following potentially high-risk processes, when provided (EPs 4–5):

4. Medication management

5. Blood and blood product use

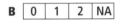

6. Through 12. Not applicable

Relevant information developed from the following activities is integrated into performance improvement initiatives. This occurs in a way consistent with any organization policies or procedures intended to preserve any confidentiality or privilege of information established by applicable law (EPs 13–17):

13. Risk management

14. Utilization management

15. Quality control

16. Infection control surveillance and reporting

B 0 1 2 NA
B 0 1 2 NA
B 0 1 2 NA
B 0 1 2 NA

---

* The Joint Commission is moving from the phrase *satisfaction with care, treatment, and services* toward the more inclusive phrase *perception of care, treatment, and services* to better measure the performance of organizations meeting the needs, expectations, and concerns of patients. By using this term, the organization will be prompted to assess not only patients' and/or families' satisfaction with care, treatment, or services, but also whether the organization meets their needs and expectations.

B | 0 | 1 | 2 | NA |

B | 0 | 1 | 2 | NA |

❏ Compliant
❏ Not Compliant

17. Research, as applicable

18. Through 24. Not applicable

Ⓜ 25. **For Medicare-certified hospices only:** The hospice must also comply with CFR 418.66. *See* Appendix D in the *2006–2007 CAMHC* for the full text of the regulation.

Standard PI.2.20

Undesirable patterns or trends in performance are analyzed.

The standard above applies to the following services:

	HH	PC/SS	HSP	Pharm Disp	C/C Pharm	LTC Pharm	Amb Infusion	HME	CRS	RT
PI.2.20	X	X	X	X	X	X	X	X	X	X

Elements of Performance for PI.2.20

The elements of performance below apply to the following services:

	HH	PC/SS	HSP	Pharm Disp	C/C Pharm	LTC Pharm	Amb Infusion	HME	CRS	RT
EP 1	X	X	X	X	X	X	X	X	X	X
EP 2	X	X	X	X	X	X	X	X	X	X
EP 3	X	X	X	X	X	X	X	X	X	X
EP 4	X		X							
EP 5	X		X	X	X	X	X		X	
EP 6	X		X	X	X	X	X		X	
EP 9	X	X	X	X	X	X	X	X	X	X
EP 11			X³							

³ Applies to Medicare-certified home health agencies only

B | 0 | 1 | 2 | NA |

1.   Analysis is performed when data comparisons indicate that levels of performance, patterns, or trends vary substantially from those expected.

B | 0 | 1 | 2 | NA |

2.   Analysis occurs for those topics chosen by leaders as performance improvement priorities.

B | 0 | 1 | 2 | NA |

3.   Analysis is performed when undesirable variation occurs which changes priorities.

A | 0 | 1 | 2 | NA |

4.   An analysis is performed for all confirmed transfusion reactions, if applicable to the organization.

A | 0 | 1 | 2 | NA |

5.   An analysis is performed for all serious adverse drug events, if applicable and as defined by the organization.

A | 0 | 1 | 2 | NA |

6.   An analysis is performed for all significant medication errors, if applicable and as defined by the organization.

7.   Not applicable

8.   Not applicable

A | 0 | 1 | 2 | NA |

9.   An analysis is performed for hazardous conditions.*

10. Not applicable

B | 0 | 1 | 2 | NA |

Ⓜ 11. **For Medicare-certified hospices only:** The hospice must also comply with CFR 418.66. *See* Appendix D in the *2006–2007 CAMHC* for the full text of the regulation.

* Any set of circumstances, defined by the organization (exclusive of the disease or condition for which the individual is being treated), which significantly increases the likelihood of a serious adverse outcome.

Standard PI.2.30

Processes for identifying and managing sentinel events are defined and implemented.

❏ Compliant
❏ Not Compliant

The standard above applies to the following services:

	HH	PC/SS	HSP	Pharm Disp	C/C Pharm	LTC Pharm	Amb Infusion	HME	CRS	RT
PI.2.30	X	X	X	X	X	X	X	X	X	X

Rationale for PI.2.30

Identifying, reporting, analyzing, and managing sentinel events can help the organization to prevent such incidents. Leaders define and implement such a program as part of the process to measure, assess, and improve the organization's performance.

Elements of Performance for PI.2.30

The elements of performance below apply to the following services:

	HH	PC/SS	HSP	Pharm Disp	C/C Pharm	LTC Pharm	Amb Infusion	HME	CRS	RT
EP 1	X	X	X	X	X	X	X	X	X	X
EP 2	X	X	X	X	X	X	X	X	X	X
EP 3	X	X	X	X	X	X	X	X	X	X
EP 4	X	X	X	X	X	X	X	X	X	X
EP 5	X	X	X	X	X	X	X	X	X	X
EP 6			X[3]							

[3] Applies to Medicare-certified hospices only

1. Processes for identifying and managing sentinel events include defining "sentinel event" and communicating this definition throughout the organization. (At a minimum, the organization's definition includes those events subject to review under the Joint Commission's Sentinel Event Policy as published in the *2006–2007 CAMHC* and may include any process variation which does not affect the outcome or result in an adverse event, but for which a recurrence carries significant chance of a serious adverse outcome or result in an adverse event, often referred to as a "near miss.")

    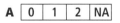

2. Processes for identifying and managing sentinel events include reporting sentinel events through established channels in the organization and, as appropriate, to external agencies in accordance with law and regulation.

    A [0 | 1 | 2 | NA]

3. Processes for identifying and managing sentinel events include conducting thorough and credible root cause analyses that focus on process and system factors.

    B [0 | 1 | 2 | NA]

4. Processes for identifying and managing sentinel events include creating, documenting, and implementing a risk-reduction strategy and action plan that includes measuring the effectiveness of process and system improvements to reduce risk.

    B [0 | 1 | 2 | NA]

5. The processes are implemented.

    B [0 | 1 | 2 | NA]

Ⓜ 6. **For Medicare-certified hospices only:** The hospice must also comply with CFR 418.66. *See* Appendix D in the *2006–2007 CAMHC* for the full text of the regulation.

    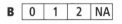

❏ Compliant
❏ Not Compliant

Standard PI.3.20

An ongoing, proactive program for identifying and reducing unanticipated adverse events and safety risks to patients is defined and implemented.

The standard above applies to the following services:

	HH	PC/SS	HSP	Pharm Disp	C/C Pharm	LTC Pharm	Amb Infusion	HME	CRS	RT
PI.3.20	X	X	X	X	X	X	X	X	X	X

Rationale for PI.3.20

Organizations should proactively seek to identify and reduce risks to the safety of patients. Such initiatives have the obvious advantage of preventing adverse events rather than simply reacting when they occur. This approach also avoids the barriers to understanding created by hindsight bias and the fear of disclosure, embarrassment, blame, and punishment that can happen after an event.

Elements of Performance for PI.3.20

The elements of performance below apply to the following services:

	HH	PC/SS	HSP	Pharm Disp	C/C Pharm	LTC Pharm	Amb Infusion	HME	CRS	RT
EP 1	X	X	X	X	X	X	X	X	X	X
EP 2	X	X	X	X	X	X	X	X	X	X
EP 3	X	X	X	X	X	X	X	X	X	X
EP 4	X	X	X	X	X	X	X	X	X	X
EP 5	X	X	X	X	X	X	X	X	X	X
EP 6	X	X	X	X	X	X	X	X	X	X
EP 7	X	X	X	X	X	X	X	X	X	X
EP 8	X	X	X	X	X	X	X	X	X	X
EP 9	X	X	X	X	X	X	X	X	X	X
EP 10			X[3]							

[3] Applies to Medicare-certified home health agencies only

The following proactive activities to reduce risks to patients are conducted (EPs 1–9):

A 0 1 2 NA

1. Selecting a high-risk process* to be analyzed (at least one high-risk process is chosen annually[†]—the choice should be based in part on information published periodically by the Joint Commission about the most frequent sentinel events and risks)

B 0 1 2 NA

2. Describing the chosen process (for example, through the use of a flowchart)

B 0 1 2 NA

3. Identifying the ways in which the process could break down[‡] or fail to perform its desired function

* **High-risk process** A process that if not planned and/or implemented correctly, has a significant potential for impacting the safety of the patient.

[†] On rare occasions, the organization may determine that it has no high-risk processes to be analyzed due to the nature of the care, treatment, and services provided (for example, a home medical equipment service provider that only delivers commodes). If this situation occurs, the organization must document on an annual basis that it has determined there are no high-risk processes as well as the reasons for the determination. Additionally, there may be rare occasions when the organization has a limited number of high-risk processes due to the nature of the care, treatment, or services provided. In those instances, the organization can re-analyze a high-risk process, provided that all identified high-risk processes related to the care, treatment, and services provided have been reviewed.

[‡] The ways in which a process could break down or fail to perform its desired function are many times referred to as "the failure modes".

4. Identifying the possible effects that a breakdown or failure of the process could have on patients and the seriousness of the possible effects

B [0 | 1 | 2 | NA]

5. Prioritizing the potential process breakdowns or failures

B [0 | 1 | 2 | NA]

6. Determining why the prioritized breakdowns or failures could occur, which may include performing a hypothetical root cause analysis

B [0 | 1 | 2 | NA]

7. Redesigning the process and/or underlying systems to minimize the risk of the effects on patients

B [0 | 1 | 2 | NA]

8. Testing and implementing the redesigned process

B [0 | 1 | 2 | NA]

9. Monitoring the effectiveness of the redesigned process

B [0 | 1 | 2 | NA]

Ⓜ 10. **For Medicare-certified hospices only:** The hospice must also comply with CFR 418.66. *See* Appendix D in the *2006–2007 CAMHC* for the full text of the regulation.

B [0 | 1 | 2 | NA]

Standard LD.4.20

New or modified services or processes are designed well.

❑ Compliant
❑ Not Compliant

The standard above applies to the following services:

	HH	PC/SS	HSP	Pharm Disp	C/C Pharm	LTC Pharm	Amb Infusion	HME	CRS	RT
LD.4.20	X	X	X	X	X	X	X	X	X	X

Elements of Performance for LD.4.20

The elements of performance below apply to the following services:

	HH	PC/SS	HSP	Pharm Disp	C/C Pharm	LTC Pharm	Amb Infusion	HME	CRS	RT
EP 1	X	X	X	X	X	X	X	X	X	X
EP 2	X	X	X	X	X	X	X	X	X	X
EP 3	X	X	X	X	X	X	X	X	X	X
EP 4	X	X	X	X	X	X	X	X	X	X
EP 5	X	X	X	X	X	X	X	X	X	X
EP 6	X	X	X	X	X	X	X	X	X	X
EP 7	X	X	X	X	X	X	X	X	X	X

The design of new or modified services or processes incorporates the following (EPs 1–6):

1. The needs and expectations of patients, staff, and others

B [0 | 1 | 2 | NA]

2. The results of performance improvement activities, when available

B [0 | 1 | 2 | NA]

3. Information about potential risks to patients, when available

B [0 | 1 | 2 | NA]

4. Current knowledge, when available and relevant (for example, practice guidelines, successful practices, information from relevant literature and clinical standards)

B [0 | 1 | 2 | NA]

5. Information about sentinel events, when available and relevant

B [0 | 1 | 2 | NA]

6. Testing and analysis to determine whether the proposed design or redesign is an improvement

B [0 | 1 | 2 | NA]

7. The leaders collaborate with staff and appropriate stakeholders to design services.

B [0 | 1 | 2 | NA]

Scoring Grid

0	Insufficient compliance
1	Partial compliance
2	Satisfactory compliance
NA	Not applicable

❑ Compliant
❑ Not Compliant

Standard LD.4.40

The leaders ensure that an integrated patient safety program is implemented throughout the organization.

The standard above applies to the following services:

	HH	PC/SS	HSP	Pharm Disp	C/C Pharm	LTC Pharm	Amb Infusion	HME	CRS	RT
LD.4.40	X	X	X	X	X	X	X	X	X	X

Rationale for LD.4.40

The leaders should work to foster a safe environment throughout the organization by integrating safety priorities into all relevant organization processes, functions, and services. In pursuit of this effort, a patient safety program can work to improve safety by reducing the risk of system or process failures. As part of its responsibility to communicate objectives and coordinate efforts to integrate patient care and support services throughout the organization and with contracted services, leadership takes the lead in developing, implementing, and overseeing a patient safety program.

The standard does not require the creation of new structures or "offices" in the organization; rather, the standard emphasizes the need to integrate all patient-safety activities, both existing and newly created, with the organization's leadership identified as accountable for this integration.

It is also critical that the organization, when establishing a patient safety program, integrate the roles and responsibilities of the patient and his or her family in reducing unanticipated adverse events and/or unanticipated adverse outcomes by providing sufficient and appropriate information about risks related to the care or services provided, instructions on minimizing those risks, and the consequences of not following such risk reduction instructions.

Elements of Performance for LD.4.40

The elements of performance below apply to the following services:

	HH	PC/SS	HSP	Pharm Disp	C/C Pharm	LTC Pharm	Amb Infusion	HME	CRS	RT
EP 1	X	X	X	X	X	X	X	X	X	X
EP 2	X	X	X	X	X	X	X	X	X	X
EP 3	X	X	X	X	X	X	X	X	X	X
EP 4	X	X	X	X	X	X	X	X	X	X
EP 5	X	X	X	X	X	X	X	X	X	X
EP 6	X	X	X	X	X	X	X	X	X	X
EP 7	X	X	X	X	X	X	X	X	X	X
EP 8	X	X	X	X	X	X	X	X	X	X

The patient safety program includes the following (EPs 1–8):

B | 0 | 1 | 2 | NA |

1. One or more qualified individuals or an interdisciplinary group assigned to manage the organizationwide safety program

B | 0 | 1 | 2 | NA |

2. Definition of the scope of the program's oversight, typically ranging from no-harm, frequently occurring "slips" to sentinel events with serious adverse outcomes

B | 0 | 1 | 2 | NA |

3. Integration into and participation of all components of the organization into the organizationwide program

B | 0 | 1 | 2 | NA |

4. Procedures for immediately responding to system or process failures, including care, treatment, or services for the affected individual(s), containing risk to others, and preserving factual information for subsequent analysis

B | 0 | 1 | 2 | NA |

5. Clear systems for internal and external reporting of information about system or process failures

6. Defined responses to various types of unanticipated adverse events and processes for conducting proactive risk assessment/risk reduction activities

B [0 | 1 | 2 | NA]

7. Defined support systems* for staff members who have been involved in a sentinel event

B [0 | 1 | 2 | NA]

8. Reports, at least annually, to the organization's governance or authority on system or process failures and actions taken to improve safety, both proactively and in response to actual occurrences

A [0 | 1 | 2 | NA]

Standard EC.9.10

The organization monitors conditions in the environment.

❑ Compliant
❑ Not Compliant

The standard above applies to the following services:

	HH	PC/SS	HSP	Pharm Disp	C/C Pharm	LTC Pharm	Amb Infusion	HME	CRS	RT
EC.9.10	X	X	X	X	X	X	X	X	X	X

Elements of Performance for EC.9.10

The elements of performance below apply to the following services:

	HH	PC/SS	HSP	Pharm Disp	C/C Pharm	LTC Pharm	Amb Infusion	HME	CRS	RT
EP 6	X	X	X	X	X	X	X	X	X	X
EP 7	X	X	X	X	X	X	X	X	X	X
EP 8	X	X	X	X	X	X	X	X	X	X
EP 9	X	X	X	X	X	X	X	X	X	X
EP 10	X	X	X	X	X	X	X	X	X	X

1. Through 5. Not applicable

6. The organization develops and uses a system for reporting, tracking, and documenting unexpected incidents, including staff and patient accidents, errors, unanticipated deaths and other events, injuries, and safety hazards related to the environment, and the care and services provided.

B [0 | 1 | 2 | NA]

Ⓜ 7. The organization reports, tracks, and documents these incidents whether or not the incident resulted in a bad outcome for a patient or staff member.

C [0 | 1 | 2 | NA]

Ⓜ 8. The organization defines specific criteria for the type(s) of accidents, injuries, and safety hazards to be reported.

C [0 | 1 | 2 | NA]

Ⓜ 9. The organization:
  - Reports all hazardous materials and waste spills, exposures, and other incidents
  - Reports utility systems management problems, failures, or user errors
  - Documents reports of accidents, injuries, and safety hazards

C [0 | 1 | 2 | NA]

10. Environmental safety monitoring and response activities are communicated to the patient safety program required in the "Leadership" chapter of the *2006–2007 CAMHC*.

B [0 | 1 | 2 | NA]

---

* Support systems provide individuals with additional help and support, as well as additional resources through the human resources function or an employee assistance program. Support systems recognize that conscientious health care workers who are involved in sentinel events are themselves victims of the event and require support. Support systems also focus on the process rather than blaming the involved individuals.

❏ Compliant
❏ Not Compliant

Standard EC.9.20

The organization analyzes identified environment issues and develops recommendations for resolving them.

The standard above applies to the following services:

	HH	PC/SS	HSP	Pharm Disp	C/C Pharm	LTC Pharm	Amb Infusion	HME	CRS	RT
EC.9.20	X	X	X	X	X	X	X	X	X	X

Elements of Performance for EC.9.20

The elements of performance below apply to the following services:

	HH	PC/SS	HSP	Pharm Disp	C/C Pharm	LTC Pharm	Amb Infusion	HME	CRS	RT
EP 7	X	X	X	X	X	X	X	X	X	X
EP 9	X	X	X	X	X	X	X	X	X	X

1. Through 6. Not applicable

C [0 | 1 | 2 | NA]

Ⓜ 7.   The organization analyzes identified environment issues and develops recommendations for resolving them. The organization does the following:
- Investigates accidents, errors, and injuries and their outcomes
- Investigates all hazardous materials and waste spills, exposures, and other incidents
- Investigates utility systems management problems, failures, or user errors
- Reports incidents and corrective actions
- Documents investigations of accidents, injuries, and safety hazards
- Keeps track of investigation results
- Identifies problematic trends

8.   Not applicable

B [0 | 1 | 2 | NA]

9.   Recommendations for resolving environmental safety issues are communicated, when appropriate, to those responsible for managing the patient safety program required in the "Leadership" chapter of the *2006–2007 CAMHC*.

❏ Compliant
❏ Not Compliant

Standard EC.9.30

The organization improves the environment of care.

The standard above applies to the following services:

	HH	PC/SS	HSP	Pharm Disp	C/C Pharm	LTC Pharm	Amb Infusion	HME	CRS	RT
EC.9.30			X				X			X

Elements of Performance for EC.9.30

The elements of performance below apply to the following services:

	HH	PC/SS	HSP	Pharm Disp	C/C Pharm	LTC Pharm	Amb Infusion	HME	CRS	RT
EP 1			X[3]				X			X[3]
EP 2			X[3]				X			X[3]

[3] Applies to facility-based services only

B [0 | 1 | 2 | NA]
B [0 | 1 | 2 | NA]

1.   Appropriate staff participates in implementing recommendations.

2.   Appropriate staff monitors the effectiveness of the recommendation's implementation.

Standard HR.2.30

Ongoing education, including in-services, training, and other activities, maintains and improves competence.

❏ Compliant
❏ Not Compliant

The standard above applies to the following services:

	HH	PC/SS	HSP	Pharm Disp	C/C Pharm	LTC Pharm	Amb Infusion	HME	CRS	RT
HR.2.30	X	X	X	X	X	X	X	X	X	X

Elements of Performance for HR.2.30

The elements of performance below apply to the following services:

	HH	PC/SS	HSP	Pharm Disp	C/C Pharm	LTC Pharm	Amb Infusion	HME	CRS	RT
EP 1	X	X	X	X	X	X	X	X	X	X
EP 2	X	X	X	X	X	X	X	X	X	X
EP 3	X	X	X	X	X	X	X	X	X	X
EP 4	X	X	X	X	X	X	X	X	X	X
EP 5	X	X	X	X	X	X	X	X	X	X
EP 6	X	X	X	X	X	X	X	X	X	X
EP 7	X	X	X	X	X	X	X	X	X	X
EP 8	X	X	X	X	X	X	X	X	X	X
EP 17	X	X	X	X	X	X	X	X	X	X
EP 18	X*									
EP 19			X[3]							

[3] Applies to Medicare-certified home health agencies only
* Applies to Medicare-certified hospices only

The following occurs for staff, students, and volunteers providing care, treatment, and services (EPs 1–8):

1. Training occurs when job responsibilities or duties change   **B** ☐0 ☐1 ☐2 ☐NA

Ⓜ 2. Participation in ongoing in-services, training, or other activities occurs to increase staff, student, or volunteer knowledge of work-related issues   **C** ☐0 ☐1 ☐2 ☐NA

Ⓜ 3. Ongoing in-services and other education and training are appropriate to the needs of the population(s) served and comply with law and regulation   **C** ☐0 ☐1 ☐2 ☐NA

Ⓜ 4. Ongoing in-services, training, or other activities emphasize specific job-related aspects of safety and infection prevention and control   **C** ☐0 ☐1 ☐2 ☐NA

Ⓜ 5. Ongoing in-services, training, or other education incorporate methods of team training, when appropriate   **C** ☐0 ☐1 ☐2 ☐NA

Ⓜ 6. Ongoing in-services, training, or other education reinforce the need and ways to report unanticipated adverse events   **C** ☐0 ☐1 ☐2 ☐NA

Ⓜ 7. Ongoing in-services or other education are offered in response to learning needs identified through performance improvement findings and other data analysis (that is, data from staff surveys, performance evaluations, or other needs assessments)   **C** ☐0 ☐1 ☐2 ☐NA

Ⓜ 8. Ongoing education is documented   **C** ☐0 ☐1 ☐2 ☐NA

9. Through 16. Not applicable

Scoring Grid

0   Insufficient compliance
1   Partial compliance
2   Satisfactory compliance
NA Not applicable

 C   0   1   2   NA

 B   0   1   2   NA

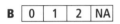 B   0   1   2   NA

❏ Compliant
❏ Not Compliant

Ⓜ 17. When patient assignments change, the organization familiarizes newly assigned staff or volunteers with the physical, psychosocial, and environmental aspects of care, treatment, and services, including patient needs; their specific responsibilities; and the specific care, treatment, and services they are to provide.*

Ⓜ 18. **For Medicare-certified home health agencies only:** The home health agency must also comply with CFRs 484.30a, 484.32, 484.32a, 484.34, 484.36a, 484.36b, 484.36b2iii, 484.36b3. *See* Appendix C in the *2006–2007 CAMHC* for the full text of the regulations.

Ⓜ 19. **For Medicare-certified hospices only:** The hospice must also comply with CFRs 418.64, 418.70a. *See* Appendix D in the *2006–2007 CAMHC* for the full text of the regulations.

Standard IM.1.10

The organization plans and designs information management processes to meet internal and external information needs.

The standard above applies to the following services:

	HH	PC/SS	HSP	Pharm Disp	C/C Pharm	LTC Pharm	Amb Infusion	HME	CRS	RT
IM.1.10	X	X	X	X	X	X	X	X	X	X

Rationale for IM.1.10

Organizations vary in size, complexity, governance, structure, decision-making processes, and resources. Information management systems and processes vary accordingly. Only by first identifying the information needs can one then evaluate the extent to which they are planned for, and at what performance level the needs are being met. Planning for the management of information does not require a formal written information plan, but does require evidence of a planned approach that identifies the organization's information needs and supports its goals and objectives.

Elements of Performance for IM.1.10

The elements of performance below apply to the following services:

	HH	PC/SS	HSP	Pharm Disp	C/C Pharm	LTC Pharm	Amb Infusion	HME	CRS	RT
EP 1	X	X	X	X	X	X	X	X	X	X
EP 2	X	X	X	X	X	X	X	X	X	X
EP 3	X	X	X	X	X	X	X	X	X	X
EP 4	X	X	X	X	X	X	X	X	X	X
EP 5	X	X	X	X	X	X	X	X	X	X
EP 6	X	X	X	X	X	X	X	X	X	X

B   0   1   2   NA

1. The organization bases its information management processes on an assessment of internal and external information needs.
   - The assessment identifies the flow of information throughout an organization, including information storage and feedback mechanisms.
   - The assessment identifies the data and information needed: within and among departments, services, or programs; within and among the staff, the administration, and the governance for supporting relationships with outside services and contractors; with licensing, accrediting, and regulatory bodies; with purchasers, payers, and employers; for supporting informational needs between the organization and the patients; and for participating in research and databases.

---

* Familiarizing newly assigned staff to a patient may include verbal or written instruction and demonstration. This activity may occur in the patient's home.

2. To guide development of processes for managing information used internally and externally, the organization assesses its information management needs based on the following:

    ● Its mission
    ● Its goals
    ● Its services
    ● Staff
    ● Patient safety considerations
    ● Quality of care, treatment, and services
    ● Mode(s) of service delivery
    ● Resources
    ● Access to affordable technology
    ● Identification of barriers to effective communication among caregivers

B | 0 | 1 | 2 | NA |

3. The organization bases its management, staffing, and material resource allocations for information management on the scope and complexity of care, treatment, and services provided.

B | 0 | 1 | 2 | NA |

4. Identified staff participates in assessment, selection, integration, and use of information management systems for clinical/service and organization information.

B | 0 | 1 | 2 | NA |

5. The organization has an ongoing process to assess the needs of the organization, departments, and individuals for knowledge-based information.

B | 0 | 1 | 2 | NA |

6. The organization uses the assessment for knowledge-based information as a basis for planning.

B | 0 | 1 | 2 | NA |

Standard IM.3.10

The organization has processes in place to effectively manage information, including the capturing, reporting, processing, storing, retrieving, disseminating, and displaying of clinical/service and non-clinical data and information.

❏ Compliant
❏ Not Compliant

The standard above applies to the following services:

	HH	PC/SS	HSP	Pharm Disp	C/C Pharm	LTC Pharm	Amb Infusion	HME	CRS	RT
IM.3.10	X	X	X	X	X	X	X	X	X	X

Rationale for IM.3.10

Records resulting from data capture and report generation* are used for communication and continuity of the patient's care or financial and business operations over time. Records are also used for other purposes, including litigation and risk management activities, reimbursement, and statistics. Improved data capture and report generation systems enhance the value of the records. Potential benefits include improved patient care, quality, and safety; improved efficiency, effectiveness and reduced costs in patient care; and improved financial and business operations. To maximize the benefits of data capture and report generation, these processes exhibit the following characteristics: unique ID, accuracy, completeness, timeliness[†], interoperability[‡], retrievability[§], authentication and accountability[‖], auditability, confidentiality, and security.

---

* **Report generation** The process of analyzing, organizing, and presenting recorded information for authentication and inclusion in the patient's health care record or in financial or business records.

† **Timeliness** The time between the occurrence of an event and the availability of data about the event. Timeliness is related to the use of the data.

‡ **Interoperability** Enables authorized users to capture, share, and report information from any system, whether paper- or electronic-based.

§ **Retrievability** The capability of efficiently finding relevant information.

‖ **Accountability** All information is attributable to its source (person or device).

The processing, storing, and retrieving functions are integral to electronic, computerized, and paper-based information systems in organizations. Important considerations for these functions include data elements, data accuracy, data confidentiality, data security, data integrity, permanence of storage (the time a medium safely stores information), ease of retrievability, aggregation of information, interoperability, clinical/service practice considerations, performance improvement, and decision support processing.

A goal for information storage is to be linked or centrally organized and accessible. This could include the organization having an index identifying where the information is stored and how to access it; or, as the organization moves to electronic systems, the organization creates information systems to be interoperable within the enterprise. As more organizations automate various processes and activities, it is important to share critical data among systems. As challenges of interoperability have arisen, standards organizations for the information technology field have stepped in to develop industry standards. It is important that the organization is aware of the standards development organizations and their recommendations.

Internally and externally generated data and information are accurately disseminated to users. Access to accurate information is required to deliver, improve, analyze, and advance patient care and the systems that support health care delivery. Information is accessed and disseminated through electronic information systems or paper-based records and reports. The use of information is considered in developing forms, screen displays, and standard or ad hoc reports.

Elements of Performance for IM.3.10

The elements of performance below apply to the following services:

	HH	PC/SS	HSP	Pharm Disp	C/C Pharm	LTC Pharm	Amb Infusion	HME	CRS	RT
EP 1	X	X	X	X	X	X	X	X	X	X
EP 2	X	X	X	X	X	X	X	X	X	X
EP 3	X	X	X	X	X	X	X	X	X	X
EP 4	X	X	X	X	X	X	X	X	X	X
EP 5	X	X	X	X	X	X	X	X	X	X
EP 6	X	X	X	X	X	X	X	X	X	X
EP 7	X	X	X	X	X	X	X	X	X	X
EP 8	X	X	X	X	X	X	X	X	X	X
EP 9	X	X	X	X	X	X	X	X	X	X
EP 10	X	X	X	X	X	X	X	X	X	X
EP 11	X[3]									

[3] Applies to Medicare-certified home health agencies only

1. Information technology industry standards or organization policies are used and address the following:
    - Uniform data definitions
    - Data capture
    - Data display
    - Data transmission

Ⓜ 2. Standardize a list of abbreviations, acronyms, and symbols that are not to be used throughout the organization.

Note: *The preceding requirement is not scored here. It is scored at National Patient Safety Goal 2, requirement 2B.*

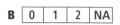

3. Minimum data sets, terminology, definitions, classifications, vocabulary, and nomenclature, including abbreviations, acronyms, and symbols, are standardized throughout the organization.

4. Quality control systems are used to monitor data content and collection activities.
    - The method used provides for timely and economical data collection with the degree of accuracy, completeness, and discrimination necessary for their intended use.
    - The method used minimizes bias in the data and regularly assesses the data's reliability, validity, and accuracy.
    - Those responsible for collecting and reviewing the data are accountable for information accuracy and completeness.

B 0 1 2 NA

5. Storage and retrieval systems are designed to support organization needs for clinical/service and organization-specific information.
    - Storage and retrieval systems are designed to balance the ability to retrieve data and information with the intended use for the data and information.
    - Storage and retrieval systems are designed to balance security and confidentiality issues with accessibility.
    - Systems for paper and electronic records are designed to reduce disruption or inaccessibility during such times as diminished staffing and scheduled and unscheduled downtimes of electronic information systems.

B 0 1 2 NA

6. Data and information are retained for sufficient time to comply with law or regulation.

A 0 1 2 NA

7. Knowledgeable staff and tools are available for collecting, retrieving, and analyzing data and their transformation into information.

B 0 1 2 NA

8. Data are organized and transformed into information in formats useful to decision makers.

B 0 1 2 NA

9. Dissemination of data and information is timely* and accurate.

B 0 1 2 NA

10. Data and information are disseminated in standard formats and methods to meet user needs and provide for retrievability and interpretation.

B 0 1 2 NA

11. **For Medicare-certified home health agencies only:** The home health agency must also comply with CFRs 484.14, 484.20a–d, 482.52a. *See* Appendix C in the *2006–2007 CAMHC* for the full text of the regulations.

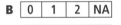

Standard IM.4.10

The information management system provides information for use in decision making.

❏ Compliant
❏ Not Compliant

The standard above applies to the following services:

	HH	PC/SS	HSP	Pharm Disp	C/C Pharm	LTC Pharm	Amb Infusion	HME	CRS	RT
IM.4.10	X	X	X	X	X	X	X	X	X	X

Rationale for IM.4.10

Information management supports timely and effective decision making at all organization levels. The information management processes support managerial and operational decisions, performance improvement activities, and patient care, treatment, and service decisions. Clinical/service and strategic decision making depends on information from multiple sources, including the patient record, knowledge-based information, comparative data/information, and aggregate data/information.

---

* **Timely** Defined by organization policy and based on the intended use of the information.

Elements of Performance for IM.4.10

The elements of performance below apply to the following services:

	HH	PC/SS	HSP	Pharm Disp	C/C Pharm	LTC Pharm	Amb Infusion	HME	CRS	RT
EP 1	X	X	X	X	X	X	X	X	X	X
EP 2	X	X	X	X	X	X	X	X	X	X
EP 3	X	X	X	X	X	X	X	X	X	X

B [0 | 1 | 2 | NA]

1. The organization has the ability to collect and aggregate data and information to support care, treatment, and service delivery and operations, including the following:
    - Individual care, treatment, and services and care, treatment, and service delivery
    - Decision making
    - Management and operations
    - Analysis of trends
    - Performance comparisons over time throughout the organization and with other organizations
    - Performance improvement
    - Infection control
    - Patient safety

B [0 | 1 | 2 | NA]

2. To support clinical/service decision making, information found in the patient record is :
    - Readily accessible
    - Accurate
    - Complete
    - Organized for retrieval of data
    - Timely*

B [0 | 1 | 2 | NA]

3. Comparative performance data and information are used for decision making, when available.

❏ Compliant
❏ Not Compliant

Standard IM.5.10

Knowledge-based information resources are readily available, current, and authoritative.

The standard above applies to the following services:

	HH	PC/SS	HSP	Pharm Disp	C/C Pharm	LTC Pharm	Amb Infusion	HME	CRS	RT
IM.5.10	X	X	X	X	X	X	X	X	X	X

Rationale for IM.5.10

Organization practitioners and staff have access to knowledge-based information* to do the following:
- Acquire and maintain the knowledge and skills needed to maintain and improve competence
- Assist with clinical/service and management decision making
- Provide appropriate information and education to patients and families
- Support performance improvement and patient safety activities
- Support the institution's educational and research needs

---

* **Knowledge-based information** A collection of stored facts, models, and information that can be used for designing and redesigning processes and for problem solving. In the context of the *2006–2007 CAMHC*, knowledge-based information is found in the clinical, scientific, and management literature.

Elements of Performance for IM.5.10

The elements of performance below apply to the following services:

	HH	PC/SS	HSP	Pharm Disp	C/C Pharm	LTC Pharm	Amb Infusion	HME	CRS	RT
EP 2	X	X	X	X	X	X	X	X	X	X
EP 3	X	X	X	X	X	X	X	X	X	X
EP 4	X	X	X	X	X	X	X	X	X	X

1. Not applicable

2. The organization provides access to knowledge-based information resources* needed by staff in any of the following forms: print, electronic, Internet, or audio.

    B [0 | 1 | 2 | NA]

3. Knowledge-based information resources are available to clinical/service staff, through electronic means, after-hours access to an in-house collection, or other methods.

    B [0 | 1 | 2 | NA]

4. The organization has a process for providing access to knowledge-based information resources when electronic systems are unavailable.

    B [0 | 1 | 2 | NA]

* Examples of knowledge-based information resources include current texts; periodicals; indexes; abstracts; reports; documents; databases; directories; discussion lists; successful practices; equipment and maintenance user manuals; standards; protocols; practice guidelines; clinical trials and other resources.

Figure 3-1. *Applicability Matrix for Ambulatory Care Safety Standards*

The grid in this figure indicates the applicability of all the ambulatory care patient safety standards and EPs. The column on the far left lists each standard, followed by its related EP. The remaining columns on the right indicate different types of ambulatory care services and/or settings. An X in an "Ambulatory Care Services/Settings" column indicates that that standard and/or EP applies to that particular service and/or setting.

The following services and settings are listed in the grid:

ASC—Ambulatory surgical centers/Office-Based Surgery Practices (Includes oral/maxillofacial surgery, podiatric surgery, ophthalmology surgery, plastic surgery, and orthopedics)

Cath. Lab—Catheterization Labs

Endoscopy—Endoscopic/Gastrointestinal Services

Diagnostic Imaging—Diagnostic Imaging Centers

Diagnostic Sleep—Diagnostic Sleep Centers and Labs

Therapeutic OT/PT—Occupational Therapy/Physical Therapy Services (Includes therapeutic services such as occupational health, rehabilitation, and infusion)

Community Health—Community Health Services

Correctional Care—Includes federal and other prisons, and immigration services

Primary Care—Includes Community Health Centers, DOD, and VA Clinics

Group Practices

Source: Adapted from Joint Commission on Accreditation of Healthcare Organizations: 2005–2006 *Comprehensive Accreditation Manual for Ambulatory Care.* Oakbrook Terrace, IL: Joint Commission, 2005. Used with permission.

continued on next page

Figure 3-1. *(continued)*

Standards and EPs	Ambulatory Care Services/Settings									
	ASCs	Cath. Labs	Endoscopy	Diagnostic Imaging	Diagnostic Sleep	Therapeutic OT/PT	Community Health	Correctional Care	Primary Care	Group Practices
RI.2.90	X	X	X	X	X	X	X	X	X	X
EP 1	X	X	X	X	X	X	X	X	X	X
EP 2	X	X	X	X	X	X	X	X	X	X
EP 3	X	X	X	X	X	X	X	X	X	X
PI.1.10	X	X	X	X	X	X	X	X	X	X
EP 1	X	X	X	X	X	X	X	X	X	X
EP 2	X	X	X	X	X	X	X	X	X	X
EP 3	X	X	X	X	X	X	X	X	X	X
EP 4	X	X	X	X	X	X	X	X	X	X
EP 5	X	X	X	X	X	X	X	X	X	X
EP 6	X	X	X	X	X	X	X	X	X	X
EP 11	X	X	X	X	X	X	X	X	X	X
EP 13	X	X	X	X	X	X	X	X	X	X
EP 14	X	X	X	X	X	X	X	X	X	X
EP 15	X	X	X	X	X	X	X	X	X	X
EP 16	X	X	X	X	X	X	X	X	X	X
EP 17	X	X	X	X	X	X	X	X	X	X
EP 23	X									
EP 24	X									
PI.2.20	X	X	X	X	X	X	X	X	X	X
EP 1	X	X	X	X	X	X	X	X	X	X
EP 2	X	X	X	X	X	X	X	X	X	X
EP 3	X	X	X	X	X	X	X	X	X	X
EP 4	X	X	X	X	X	X	X	X	X	X
EP 5	X	X	X	X	X	X	X	X	X	X
EP 6	X	X	X	X	X	X	X	X	X	X
EP 7	X	X	X	X	X	X	X	X	X	X
EP 8	X	X	X	X	X	X	X	X	X	X
EP 9	X	X	X	X	X	X	X	X	X	X
PI.2.30	X	X	X	X	X	X	X	X	X	X
EP 1	X	X	X	X	X	X	X	X	X	X
EP 2	X	X	X	X	X	X	X	X	X	X

continued on next page

Figure 3-1. *(continued)*

Standards and EPs	ASCs	Cath. Labs	Endoscopy	Diagnostic Imaging	Diagnostic Sleep	Therapeutic OT/PT	Community Health	Correctional Care	Primary Care	Group Practices
								Ambulatory Care Services/Settings		
EP 3	X	X	X	X	X	X	X	X	X	X
EP 4	X	X	X	X	X	X	X	X	X	X
EP 5	X	X	X	X	X	X	X	X	X	X
PI.3.20	X	X	X	X	X	X	X	X	X	X
EP 1	X	X	X	X	X	X	X	X	X	X
EP 2	X	X	X	X	X	X	X	X	X	X
EP 3	X	X	X	X	X	X	X	X	X	X
EP 4	X	X	X	X	X	X	X	X	X	X
EP 5	X	X	X	X	X	X	X	X	X	X
EP 6	X	X	X	X	X	X	X	X	X	X
EP 7	X	X	X	X	X	X	X	X	X	X
EP 8	X	X	X	X	X	X	X	X	X	X
EP 9	X	X	X	X	X	X	X	X	X	X
LD.4.20	X	X	X	X	X	X	X	X	X	X
EP 1	X	X	X	X	X	X	X	X	X	X
EP 2	X	X	X	X	X	X	X	X	X	X
EP 3	X	X	X	X	X	X	X	X	X	X
EP 4	X	X	X	X	X	X	X	X	X	X
EP 5	X	X	X	X	X	X	X	X	X	X
EP 6	X	X	X	X	X	X	X	X	X	X
EP 7	X	X	X	X	X	X	X	X	X	X
LD.4.40	X	X	X	X	X	X	X	X	X	X
EP 1	X	X	X	X	X	X	X	X	X	X
EP 2	X	X	X	X	X	X	X	X	X	X
EP 3	X	X	X	X	X	X	X	X	X	X
EP 4	X	X	X	X	X	X	X	X	X	X
EP 5	X	X	X	X	X	X	X	X	X	X
EP 6	X	X	X	X	X	X	X	X	X	X
EP 7	X	X	X	X	X	X	X	X	X	X
EP 8	X	X	X	X	X	X	X	X	X	X
EC.9.10	X	X	X	X	X	X	X	X	X	X
EP 1	X	X	X	X	X	X	X	X	X	X

continued on next page

Figure 3-1. *(continued)*

Standards and EPs	Ambulatory Care Services/Settings									
	ASCs	Cath. Labs	Endoscopy	Diagnostic Imaging	Diagnostic Sleep	Therapeutic OT/PT	Community Health	Correctional Care	Primary Care	Group Practices
EP 2	X	X	X	X	X	X	X	X	X	X
EP 3	X	X	X	X	X	X	X	X	X	X
EP 4	X	X	X	X	X	X	X	X	X	X
EP 5	X	X	X	X	X	X	X	X	X	X
EP 10	X	X	X	X	X	X	X	X	X	X
EC.9.20	X	X	X	X	X	X	X	X	X	X
EP 1	X	X	X	X	X	X	X	X	X	X
EP 3	X	X	X	X	X	X	X	X	X	X
EP 4	X	X	X	X	X	X	X	X	X	X
EP 5	X	X	X	X	X	X	X	X	X	X
EP 6	X	X	X	X	X	X	X	X	X	X
EP 8	X	X	X	X	X	X	X	X	X	X
EP 9	X	X	X	X	X	X	X	X	X	X
EC.9.30	X	X	X	X	X	X	X	X	X	X
EP 1	X	X	X	X	X	X	X	X	X	X
EP 2	X	X	X	X	X	X	X	X	X	X
EP 3	X	X	X	X	X	X	X	X	X	X
EP 5	X	X	X	X	X	X	X	X	X	X
HR.2.30	X	X	X	X	X	X	X	X	X	X
EP 1	X	X	X	X	X	X	X	X	X	X
EP 2	X	X	X	X	X	X	X	X	X	X
EP 3	X	X	X	X	X	X	X	X	X	X
EP 4	X	X	X	X	X	X	X	X	X	X
EP 5	X	X	X	X	X	X	X	X	X	X
EP 6	X	X	X	X	X	X	X	X	X	X
EP 7	X	X	X	X	X	X	X	X	X	X
EP 8	X	X	X	X	X	X	X	X	X	X
IM.1.10	X	X	X	X	X	X	X	X	X	X
EP 1	X	X	X	X	X	X	X	X	X	X
EP 2	X	X	X	X	X	X	X	X	X	X
EP 3	X	X	X	X	X	X	X	X	X	X
EP 4	X	X	X	X	X	X	X	X	X	X

continued on next page

Figure 3-1. *(continued)*

Standards and EPs	Ambulatory Care Services/Settings									
	ASCs	Cath. Labs	Endoscopy	Diagnostic Imaging	Diagnostic Sleep	Therapeutic OT/PT	Community Health	Correctional Care	Primary Care	Group Practices
EP 5	X	X	X	X	X	X	X	X	X	X
IM.3.10	X	X	X	X	X	X	X	X	X	X
EP 1	X	X	X	X	X	X	X	X	X	X
EP 2	X	X	X	X	X	X	X	X	X	X
EP 3	X	X	X	X	X	X	X	X	X	X
EP 4	X	X	X	X	X	X	X	X	X	X
EP 5	X	X	X	X	X	X	X	X	X	X
EP 6	X	X	X	X	X	X	X	X	X	X
EP 7	X	X	X	X	X	X	X	X	X	X
EP 8	X	X	X	X	X	X	X	X	X	X
EP 9	X	X	X	X	X	X	X	X	X	X
EP 10	X	X	X	X	X	X	X	X	X	X
EP 11	X	X	X	X	X	X	X	X	X	X
IM.4.10	X	X	X	X	X	X	X	X	X	X
EP 1	X	X	X	X	X	X	X	X	X	X
EP 2	X	X	X	X	X	X	X	X	X	X
EP 3	X	X	X	X	X	X	X	X	X	X
EP 4	X	X	X	X	X	X	X	X	X	X
EP 5	X	X	X	X	X	X	X	X	X	X
EP 6	X	X	X	X	X	X	X	X	X	X
EP 7	X	X	X	X	X	X	X	X	X	X
IM.5.10	X	X	X	X	X	X	X	X	X	X
EP 1	X	X	X	X	X	X	X	X	X	X
EP 2	X	X	X	X	X	X	X	X	X	X
EP 3	X	X	X	X	X	X	X	X	X	X
EP 4	X	X	X	X	X	X	X	X	X	X

CHAPTER FOUR

Patient Safety–Related Requirements in Other Joint Commission Standards

Developing a safety program involves more than just examining the safety standards addressed in Chapter 3. Many other Joint Commission standards also address safety issues. In fact, almost half of Joint Commission standards are directly related to safety, addressing such issues as the following:

- Provision of care, treatment, and services

- Medication management

- Infection control

- Laboratory issues

- Staffing effectiveness

This chapter discusses how compliance with patient safety–related requirements in the "Provision of Care, Treatment, and Services" (PC), "Medication Management" (MM), and "Surveillance, Prevention, and Control of Infection" (IC) chapters can help organizations with their proactive risk reduction efforts and ultimately enhance patient safety. In addition, safety-related issues in the laboratory setting and staffing effectiveness standards are discussed.

Provision of Care, Treatment, and Services

Thorough and timely patient assessment and reassessment are critical to patient safety. As outlined in all Joint Commission accreditation manuals, the goal of assessment is to determine the care, treatment, and services required to meet a patient's needs, both initially and as the patient's needs change in response to care, treatment, and services. During the initial assessment, the patient's physical, psychological, social, nutritional, functional, and pain status should be assessed by qualified staff.

Five key processes for ensuring safe provision of care are evident in the PC safety-related standards; these processes should be familiar to health care staff.

Five Key Activities

Safe care comes from ensuring five key activities. The *first* is accepting for care, treatment, and services only those individuals whose identified care, treatment, and service needs can be met by the organization. The *second* is ensuring that staff thoroughly assesses and reassesses the individual to identify the appropriate care, treatment, and services to meet the individual's initial needs as well as his or her changing needs while in the setting. The *third* is ensuring that the organization develops the right plan of care for the individual—a plan that is appropriate to address the individual's specific and unique needs—and that the plan is revised as needed. The *fourth* is providing planned and appropriate interventions safely in settings that are responsive to specific individual needs. The *fifth* is ensuring that continuity of care is maintained when the individual is discharged or transferred.

Critical to patient safety and care quality, these activities are central to what health care staff do. What happens during the course of mere minutes in an emergency department, hours or days on a general care unit, or months and years in a long term care facility must revolve around making sure that a patient's needs are identified and met. Moreover, patient needs continually change. For example, a patient enters the emergency department after having suffered a heart attack. His diabetes is out of control, he is non-compliant with his antihypertension medications, and he has very distinct nutritional needs. Getting that patient stabilized will be the primary focus of the initial care process. Once he's stable, other care needs can be addressed.

Improving Entry to Care

Organizations can do the following to improve patients' entry to care.

■ *Clearly define the scope of services and provide only care, treatment, and services within this scope.* The scope should reflect the organization's mission and should be as broad or as narrow as appropriate to that mission.

■ *Establish criteria to determine entry eligibility and use criteria consistently.* Criteria for eligibility should reflect the organization's scope of services and be applied consistently to all individuals presenting at the care entry point. If the organization cannot meet a patient's critical care need(s), the patient must be referred or transferred to another organization that can meet his or her need(s). If the organization can meet the patient's need(s) and admits the patient, but then "noncritical" care needs present for which the organization cannot provide services, upon discharge the patient must be referred for follow-up care or have arrangements made with other facilities.

Improving Assessment and Reassessment

Inadequate patient assessment can lead to longer lengths of stay, unnecessary treatment, and, at times more seriously, the omission of necessary treatment. The following tips can help prevent patient safety compromise.

■ *Develop or select screening and assessment tools specific to the population(s) served.* Regularly review these tools. Staff should routinely review the effectiveness of assessment and screening tools. The initial assessment tool should serve as a screen that, when tied into a scoring mechanism, triggers an in-depth assessment. Tools must be tested regularly.

■ *When indicated, use a combination of assessment techniques.* The use of different assessment techniques, such as observation or communication with the individual and family, helps to provide as thorough an assessment as possible.

Improving Care Planning and Provision

To ensure patient safety, the care plan must address the patient's specific needs and the multidisciplinary interventions to meet such needs. Appropriate care must then be provided in a timely fashion. Care planning involves more than generating a statement of goals; it involves actively changing the goals, as needed, in response to the patient's needs and response to treatment. Consider the following tips.

■ *Ensure proper timing for developing the plan of care and regularly review and revise it, as needed.* The timing of the plan of care's development can create patient safety problems. A plan that is developed too early after an individual's entry for care may not include critical information (for example, fall risk as a result of dizziness caused by a new medication) gathered later during the patient's stay.

■ *Use a comprehensive interdisciplinary team and ensure prioritization of care needs and goals.* A comprehensive interdisciplinary care plan includes input from all disciplines on the most important needs and goals for each patient. Agreement on how to prioritize these goals determines how caregivers will address each goal during the patient's stay. Caregiver observations may call attention to changing needs and the necessity of reprioritizing as treatment progresses.

Improving Discharge Planning

Proper discharge planning helps prevent patient injury. For example, to reduce the likelihood of an injurious fall, the discharge plan for a frail elderly patient following treatment for pneumonia should include a referral for home or rehabilitative care. Other tips include the following:

■ *Ensure adequate assessment for discharge needs.* Along with information required to diagnose and treat the patient, the organization must obtain information about the patient's abilities and needs after release from the organization.

■ *Ensure regular reassessment of discharge needs.* Discharge planning is not a one-time event in the assessment process. Discharge planning should begin at admission or entry and continue throughout the patient's stay.

■ *Reconcile patient medications.* Develop a process for obtaining and documenting a complete list of the patient's medication. *See* pages 46–48 in Chapter 2 for more information.

The Assessment-Safety Link

Patient safety and complete and timely assessment are inextricably linked. Inadequate patient assessment or reassessment ranks third among the most frequently cited root causes of all sentinel events reported to the Joint Commission. In addition, approximately 82% of the organizations that reported a patient suicide and 75% of organizations that reported a restraint-related death cited incomplete patient assessment as a root cause.* Thorough assessment can help an organization proactively identify risks and take steps to avoid such risks. Complying with the assessment-related standards helps organizations establish a culture to reduce errors by identifying potential issues with patients before the issues become problems. This type of culture enhances patient safety and reduces the likelihood of sentinel events.

Avoiding Sentinel Events

Several of the most frequently reported sentinel events have root causes linked to inadequate patient assessment. Following is a discussion of specific sentinel events with suggestions on how organizations can proactively work to minimize risks associated with these sentinel events.

Suicide

To help prevent patient suicides, organizations should examine their assessment procedures. Assessment findings can highlight an individual's risk for suicide and determine the degree of observation needed. Suicide screening should be part of both initial assessments and reassessments (as needed). Organization policies may need to be updated to ensure that criteria and procedures for patient observation are consistently applied.

Also, organizations should review their policies dealing with the transfer of information from one setting or unit to another. The periods immediately following admission and immediately preceding discharge from a specific area can increase the level of risk dramatically, and all staff should be aware of an individual's suicide risk potential.

When revising an assessment tool to include the assessment for suicide potential, organizations should look at common risk factors. Youths, the medically ill, specific population groups (such as Native Americans, Alaskan Natives, and African American males between 15 and 19 years of age), individuals with mental and substance abuse disorders, and the elderly often account for the highest number of suicides.[1] Factors such as social isolation and a lack of emotional support, worries about finances or work, a history of gambling or alcohol/substance abuse, easy access to a firearm or potentially lethal medicines, psychiatric illness and personality disorders, or a family history of suicide may exacerbate the risk of suicide even more. In addition to including common risk factors on assessment forms, organizations should look at the data collected within their own facility regarding completed and attempted suicides. By knowing the risk factors specific to a population(s), organizations can revise their assessment tools for greater efficiency.

Wrong Site, Wrong Person, Wrong Procedure Surgery

The lack of a thorough preoperative assessment is frequently a contributing factor to wrong site surgery. Failure to review the medical record or imaging studies in the immediate preoperative period is often involved. The surgical site and procedure must be clearly noted in the assessment. A "total knee replacement" statement in the chart does not indicate the side of the procedure. Laterality is often the key element in describing the surgical site. To prevent a wrong site surgery sentinel event, staff must ensure proper identification of the surgical site and procedure in each preoperative assessment and ask questions if information is not clear. Each preoperative assessment must also include information from the informed consent, medical record, imaging studies, and other sources in verifying the site. Staff should request such information if it is not available. Additional tips to help organizations prevent wrong site, wrong procedure, and wrong patient surgery can be found in Chapter 2 under the discussion of the Universal Protocol National Patient Safety Goal.

---

* As of September 30, 2005. For updated sentinel event statistics, please visit the Joint Commission's Web site at http://www.jointcommission.org/SentinelEvents/Statistics/.

Operative and Postoperative Complications

Thorough and complete assessment can help organizations prevent interoperative and postoperative complications. These terms can cover a multitude of situations and degrees of seriousness. However, many such events that have been reported to the Joint Commission have resulted in serious injury or death. All reports were from acute care facilities, and the events occurred during the anesthesia induction period, the intraoperative procedure period, the postanesthesia recovery period, and the postprocedure period. Most of the incidents did not involve emergency procedures.

Root cause analyses of these sentinel events indicated that well over half of them were primarily the result of incomplete communication among staff and/or physicians as well as failure to follow established procedures. Other causal factors included the unavailability of necessary personnel, incomplete preoperative assessments, a lack of proper clinical training for certain procedures, inconsistent postoperative monitoring, staff failure to question inappropriate orders, and inadequate supervision of staff.

To help avoid operative and postoperative complications, organizations should perform complete, timely, and accurate assessments. These assessments include pre-, intra- and postoperative monitoring. Assessments need to be done regularly by competent personnel according to each patient's needs and regardless of the setting.

In addition to properly assessing the patient, organizations should clearly define and establish direct paths of communication among all caregivers. Clearly defining and establishing direct paths of communication relates not only to consistent procedures, but also to encouraging a culture in which all members of the health care team are able to express opinions and ask questions.

Transfusion Errors

Transfusion errors can be prevented through proper assessment, as well as proper patient identification. Initial patient assessment ensures that a patient should actually receive blood. After the blood is administered, ongoing monitoring and assessment ensure that any adverse events are identified and treated promptly and appropriately.

Staff must be able to recognize the signs and symptoms of a transfusion reaction. Failure to do so can result in treatment delay and, in the worst case, a sentinel event.

Fall Assessment/Prevention

Proper assessment reduces the likelihood of injuries and deaths that result from falls. The first task in preventing falls is to correctly and completely assess a patient's risk of falling. Many organizations build this risk assessment into the initial assessment performed on admission. Risk factors include the following:

- A history of previous falls

- Mental status

- Lack of or inadequate communication

- Sensory and auditory deficits

- Medications

- Urinary alterations

- Emotional upset

Staff should consider all medications as part of the assessment and reassessment processes, including all prescription medications, over-the-counter drugs, and supplements the patient is taking. They should also document medication allergies and history of substance abuse, including abuse of tranquilizers or other prescription drugs.

Different assessment techniques, such as observation or communication with the individual and family, help to provide as thorough an assessment as possible. Communication with family members and significant others is critical to thorough assessment of fall risk. Staff should inform family members about factors that increase fall risk and inquire about the presence of any such factors.

Regular reassessment ensures success of interventions to address increased fall risk. Among other changes, medication changes— including drug addictions and increased or decreased dosages—create the need for vigilant monitoring for possible new side effects. A new medication added to a patient's current medication regimen could cause dizziness, sedation, or other symptoms that place the patient at increased risk for falls. Regular staff reassessment and monitoring for behaviors indicating impaired judgment, particularly if the patient has had any sort of procedure involving anesthesia, can reduce the risk of falls.

Treatment Delays

Treatment delays can occur in practically any setting, including inpatient psychiatric facilities, ambulatory clinics, intensive care units, medical/surgical units, and patients' homes. Consider this example in which treatment delay compromised safe care: A resident in a nursing home is transferred to a nearby hospital for an outpatient procedure. The resident, who suffers from dementia, requires assistance with walking. She is admitted to the hospital after the procedure. Staff members at the hospital perform an initial assessment, but they delay performing a functional status and a reassessment. Thus, the resident's plan of care does not indicate supervision while ambulating. During the night, the resident gets up to use the bathroom and falls. She suffers a subdural hematoma and dies three days later.

In the example above, problems occurred when staff failed to perform an appropriate assessment and reassessment. Assessment standards in the PC chapter require functional assessment and reassessment at regular intervals; a patient's condition might change throughout the course of care, thus requiring different interventions. Functional assessment and reassessment are necessary to furnish information on which to base care decisions that will best meet the individual's needs. The delay in performing assessments and reassessments delayed treatment and possibly contributed to the adverse outcome.

Although frustrating, treatment delays are preventable. Organizations can reduce the likelihood of delays by doing the following:

- Ensuring complete, accurate, and timely assessment and reassessment of patients

- Including initial assessment and reassessment procedures in organization orientation and training processes including the time frames the organization has set up for initial assessments, as well as how to conduct the assessments

- Training nonclinical staff in the admitting area to become familiar with potential warning signs that might signal the need for swift intervention (or assessment) by a health care professional

Patient and Family Education

Another PC standard addressing safety requires that patients and their families be educated about their roles in reporting perceived risks to their care. To ensure this, organizations are required to outline patient and family responsibilities and to educate them about these responsibilities. Specific attention should be directed at educating patients and families about their roles in establishing a safe health care experience. The patient's family or surrogate decision maker assumes this responsibility for the patient if the patient has been found by his or her physician to be incapable of understanding his or her responsibilities, has been judged incompetent in accordance with law, or exhibits a communication barrier.

In outlining patient responsibilities, organizations should educate individuals about the following:

- The plan for care, treatment, and services

- Basic health practices and safety

- The safe and effective use of medications

- Nutrition interventions, modified diets, or oral health

- Safe and effective use of medical equipment or supplies when provided by the hospital

- Understanding pain, the risk for pain, the importance of effective pain management, the pain assessment process, and methods for pain management

- Habilitation or rehabilitation techniques to help them reach maximum independence possible

Patients should be educated about their responsibilities during the admission, registration, or intake process and as needed thereafter. This education can take place verbally, in writing, or both.

Within the home care setting, health care professionals are not present at all times so it is critical that patients and their families or caregivers receive education about any risks associated with the care, treatment, and services provided, the ways to minimize these risks, and the consequences of not following risk reduction procedures. They should also know what the expected outcomes of treatment are and how equipment is supposed to perform so they can identify problems as they arise and notify someone in the organization rather than wait until the next home care visit.

Sidebar 4-1, "Five Steps to Engage Patients in Safety," page 125, highlights key steps health care providers can take to more actively involve patients in safety. *See* page 25 in Chapter 1 for more information about SpeakUp™.

Medication Management

Medication management is one of the most important yet challenging systems in any health care organization. It pervades almost every patient experience from initial evaluation to discharge or ongoing monitoring and involves multiple disciplines throughout the organization, including pharmacy, nursing, medical staff, and therapists.

The Medication Management standards reflect the critical processes involved in medication management. Requirements also address the need for patient-specific information and processes pertaining to high-risk medications. In addition, two standards address managing medications returned to the pharmacy and prescribing medications according to an individual's needs. The first standard refers to an organization's policies and procedures (and their implementation) for medications returned to the pharmacy for any reason. Questions that might pertain to this process include the following:

- How do you determine whether the medication is suitable to be put back into stock?

- How do you dispose of the medication if it cannot be put back into stock?

- Where/how is the medication stored until staff makes this decision?

The second standard requires that only medications necessary to treat the patient's condition be prescribed. This standard requires that, for each medication prescribed, there must be a diagnosis, condition, or indication that supports the use of that medication. The reason for the prescription does not need to be listed on the original order, but it should be evident in the care-planning process or elsewhere in the patient's record and be available to all caregivers who participate in managing the patient's medications (for example, pharmacists, nurses, physicians).

Addressing Safety Through Medication Management

To provide safe, high-quality patient care, treatment, and services, systems must function well across the entire organization. There are several ways for organizations to evaluate their medication management systems to ensure patient safety is preserved. Following are some suggestions:

- Follow a sample of individual patients from admission through discharge (or ongoing monitoring for long-term treatment/maintenance) and look at medication issues at each stage. The scenario found in Sidebar 4-2 on page 127, "Tracing a Patient to Identify Medication Management Issues," shows how an organization with multiple settings might approach this type of evaluation. When choosing "tracer" patients, organizations should try to include at least one from each of the populations served, as well as those populations requiring different levels of care, treatment, and services. (For more information about tracer activities, please see pages 143–154 in Chapter 5.)

- Review a random sample of medical records for appropriate medication management. Keep the following points in mind as records are reviewed:

- Check to see that the medication profiles kept by nursing staff match those of the pharmacy and that both match what the patient is actually taking

- Whenever an order has been received by phone, make sure that it was written down and read back to the physician to verify accuracy. For tips on how to do

---

Sidebar 4-1.
Five Steps to Engage Patients in Safety

Reducing errors and improving the safety of care requires the coordinated efforts of many individuals, including patients themselves.

As another set of eyes, patients can help identify potential errors as they observe and participate in the care process. Patients can also help lessen the effects of errors that have occurred by informing clinicians of adverse outcomes so that prompt action can be taken.

The following are five key strategies to help make patients aware of and engage them in the vital role they play in receiving safe care, treatment, and services.

1. Communicate with patients about safety. Let patients know that mistakes can and do happen, but they can help prevent them. Don't scare them, but give patients an awareness and sense of importance in their task. Safety topics might include hand washing, isolation procedures, medications, normal equipment operation, lab results, illegible instructions or prescriptions, and so forth.

The key message should be to speak up with any and all questions or concerns. Engage patients: Don't just give a patient a brochure on safety, but refer to it during discussions. When a patient expresses a concern, thank him or her for being involved and double-check whether the procedure or treatment is called for in the care plan.

Distribute and review brochures or other materials about the basics of the patient's care. Generally, the more involved a patient is in his or her care and treatment, the less likely a medical error will occur.[1] During interactions with patients and families, be sensitive to cultural beliefs and practices to help avoid misunderstandings, misdiagnoses, or noncompliance.

2. Actively involve the patient in safety procedures. Engaging patients in their safety needn't be difficult, expensive, or time prohibitive. Ask patients to remind staff to identify themselves or to wash their hands before examining them. Accredited organizations are required to involve patients in marking the site for invasive procedures as part of the preprocedure process.

Urge patients to become active, involved, and informed participants on the health care team.

3. Give patients tools for safety. Hang patient safety posters in frequent stand-by areas such as elevators, cafeterias, or waiting rooms. Provide take-along tools for patients. Some ideas include the following:

- Keep a pad and pen at the bedside or in the exam room for questions or concerns

- Provide the patient with a chart outlining scheduled care

- Give out wallet cards to list medications, allergies, chronic conditions, provider contact information, and so forth

- Educate patients on common side effects and when it's important to call a physician or pharmacist

- Develop or adapt a guide for family members and friends, offering advice on how to be supportive and help monitor the patient's safety

4. Be accountable to patients. Make a commitment to be transparent with patient outcomes, good or bad. Share results on the National Patient Safety Goals. Approach errors with full, honest, and open disclosure. Following an incident, staff need to contact the family, meet to explain what happened, and offer assistance.

Invite patients to approach staff with safety concerns and foster a culture of safety that will accept this feedback as an opportunity to learn and improve, not as a criticism. Ask a consumer to sit on a safety committee. Consider introducing patient safety leadership rounds. Senior leaders can visit different areas each week or month to ask staff and patients questions about specific occurrences that week and about the factors that led to the events. This can lead to faster, broader-reaching responses to safety issues.

5. Bridge the gap between patients and providers. Train patient representatives (such as an ombudsman, a social worker, or another patient advocate) in patient safety and issues related to medical errors; publicize these representatives' services to patients and the community.

Represent patient interests on the board of trustees and key committees. Implement a patient and family advisory council to integrate the shared experiences of patients, their families, and their health care providers. Tapping in to this unique perspective can reveal a host of previously unidentified issues. The Institute for Family-Centered Care (http://www.familycenteredcare.org) has developed resources to help develop and effectively run such a council.

Reference

1. Regents of the University of Michigan: University of Michigan Health System Patient Safety Toolkit: *Improving Patient Safety in Hospitals: Turning Ideas into Action,* "Safety Curriculum" chapter. Ann Arbor, MI: UMHS Department of Public Relations and Marketing Communications. (Accessed Jan. 5, 2006 at http://www.med.umich.edu/patientsafetytoolkit.)

---

this, *see* National Patient Safety Goal #2 on pages 34–36 in Chapter 2.

- Make sure your organization has a list of abbreviations that are never to be used

- Many of these will be particularly relevant to medication orders. Determine

whether any of these abbreviations has been used, and if so, what process was followed when it was detected (for instance, clarification of the intended meaning with the prescribed). For tips on how to do this, *see* National Patient Safety Goal #2 on pages 36–37 in Chapter 2.

- Perform an internal functional review of medication management systems, tracing a path from entry through ordering, administration, storage, monitoring, and so forth. Consider the risk points and potential opportunities for error. Organizations should ask how these vulnerabilities are addressed. For example, are internal systems and processes consistent?

- Perform a proactive risk assessment on medication management processes to help anticipate problems and identify areas of improvement

Avoiding Sentinel Events

Medication errors are among the most frequently occurring types of errors for most health care organizations, primarily because a problem can occur at any stage in the process from prescribing to monitoring. Many factors contribute to these errors, but an ever-growing problem is sound-alike drugs—medications with similar names that can easily be mistaken for one another, especially when verbal orders are used. Similar drug names account for about 15% of reports made to the U.S. Pharmacopeia (USP) Medication Errors Reporting (MER) program. The confusion over similar brand and generic drug names is compounded by factors such as the following:

- Incomplete knowledge of drug names

- Newly available products

- Illegible handwriting

- Similar packaging or labeling

- Incorrect selection of a drug from a computerized list

The Joint Commission's medication management chapter includes several guidelines that can help reduce errors associated with sound-alike medications. For example, when adding medications to the organization's formulary, staff should consider the potential for dispensing errors. The names of new medications are often not checked against those already on the list; thus, no precautions are taken to ensure that mix-ups will not occur. Sometimes alternative medications that do not present nomenclature problems can be selected. If this is not possible, drugs may be grouped by category rather than alphabetically to keep products with similar-sounding names separate. Pharmacy staff can also place reminders in computer systems and reminder labels on containers to alert physicians, nurses, and pharmacists to a potential problem.

As described in Chapter 2, verbal medication orders, especially those taken by telephone, present a serious potential for sound alike errors. Because it is impossible to avoid verbal orders completely, a pharmacist's confirmation of the patient's diagnosis and review of an order before filling verbal requests (except in emergencies) can help cut down on misunderstandings. In addition, qualified personnel taking the order should write down the order (or enter it into a computer), then read it back verbatim to the practitioner who initiated it. The practitioner should then verbally confirm that the order is correct.

Joint Commission standards also call for procedures to ensure the safe and effective dispensing of medications, including pharmacist review of all prescriptions/ orders and a standardized method for labeling all medications dispensed to inpatients and outpatients. A good medication labeling system contains multiple checks at different stages of the medication process—for example, the pharmacist reviews the prescription against the order entered in the computer system and nurses check the medication package/label against the patient's chart before administering the dose.

Infection Control

Infections and infection control are more in the news today than ever before. The threat of bioterrorism, an overall increase in infectious diseases such as HIV and hepatitis, earlier discharges from acute care facilities, and staff shortages have all increased public awareness of infection control.

Health care–associated infections (HAIs) remain a serious problem in health care. Reducing the risk and preventing the spread of infection has become a safety priority and requirement for all health care organizations.

IC Standards and Patient Safety

The Joint Commission's "Surveillance, Prevention and Control of Infection" (IC)

Sidebar 4-2. Tracing a Patient to Identify Medication Management Issues

Ambulatory Care Setting

Mr. Johnson's daughter took him to a freestanding urgent care center because he was exhibiting signs of extreme disorientation, lack of coordination, and poor equilibrium. Mr. Johnson, 82, also had a bag filled with prescriptions for a variety of chronic conditions, all from different physicians and pharmacies. A preliminary diagnosis of diabetes and drug-induced disorientation was made, and staff referred Mr. Johnson to a nearby hospital for tests and further care.

Following are some questions* to ask the ambulatory staff involved in Mr. Johnson's care:

- Were all the prescriptions the patient brought in listed in the history? How did you determine which medications Mr. Johnson was actually taking? How did you provide for required medications so his schedule would not be interrupted?

- What information did you provide to the hospital to which you referred the patient? How was that information transmitted?

Hospital Setting

Mr. Johnson was admitted for glucose testing and evaluation of the various medications he was taking. He was diagnosed with new onset of diabetes and was found to be taking multiple antihypertensives, along with prescription medications for osteoarthritis and cholesterol, an over-the-counter (OTC) medication for hay fever, and an herbal supplement (St John's Wort) to combat depression. He exhibited various symptoms of increasing dementia. Insulin was prescribed for Mr. Johnson's diabetes and the attending physician and pharmacist conferred on medications that could safely be taken together for his other chronic conditions. Once he had been stabilized and he and his daughter were educated about his new prescriptions, diet, and needs, Mr. Johnson was transferred to a long term care facility.

Following are some questions to ask the hospital staff involved in Mr. Johnson's care:

- What information did you receive from the referring organization?

- How and when were Mr. Johnson's medication needs assessed and reassessed? Why were drugs X, Y, and Z prescribed?

- Are medication orders legible, complete and without any prohibited abbreviations, and authorized correctly? Are only accepted abbreviations used for medications?

- What process was followed to confirm patient identification before administering medications?

- Does the administration record match the orders in the patient record?

- How was the effectiveness of medications evaluated?

- How was Mr. Johnson's response to medications monitored?

---

* The questions in this example are specific to the patient scenario presented here. During actual tracer activities, Joint Commission surveyors will not ask standardized questions; any questions asked will be based on the care, treatment, and services a particular patient received within a particular organization.

Visit the pharmacy.

- How did you get the necessary information regarding allergies, diseases, and so on to evaluate Mr. Johnson's medication plan?

- Do the pharmacy records match the original orders and administration records for all original and revised prescriptions?

- How are these medications stored (refrigeration and so forth)?

- Was it necessary to mix the insulin? If so, what process was used to ensure correct amounts, labeling, and so on?

Go over the discharge/transfer plan.

- What education did Mr. Johnson and his daughter receive regarding the use of insulin for his diabetes?

- How was the new medication plan explained to them?

- What information was sent to the nursing home, and how was it transmitted?

Long Term Care Setting

Although Mr. Johnson's cognitive functioning was impaired, he was able to perform many activities of daily living unassisted. Long term care was needed to manage dementia and ensure that the correct medications were given on time and in the right dosage, that his blood sugar level was monitored, and that his dietary needs were met.

Following are some questions to ask the long term care staff involved in Mr. Johnson's care:

- How did you learn about Mr. Johnson's conditions and needs when he was transferred from the hospital? How did you provide for routine medications so his schedule would not be interrupted?

- How do you know the specific assessments to include in monitoring Mr. Johnson's response to his medications? For example, do you perform glucose testing at prescribed intervals and communicate this information to the pharmacy/physician?

- What medications do you store at your facility? How do you ensure security, proper temperature, and so on?

- Does Mr. Johnson exhibit any behaviors that might interfere with medication compliance (for example, holding pills under his tongue, eating too many candy bars when alone)?

Talk to staff at the pharmacy that serves the nursing home.

- How did you get the necessary information to assess Mr. Johnson's medication plan for appropriateness of drug, dose, and route, as well as allergies, diseases, and interactions before delivery of the first dose?

- How did the pharmacist get the necessary information to assess her therapy for appropriateness of drug, dose, and route, as well as allergies, diseases, and interactions before delivery of the first dose?

standards raise expectations on addressing this very serious issue in health care. Prevention of HAIs represents one of the major safety initiatives an organization can undertake, making the effective evaluation and possible redesign of existing infection prevention and control programs a priority. The Centers for Disease Control and Prevention (CDC) estimates that each year more than 2 million patients admitted to acute care hospitals, where HAIs are best documented, develop infections that were not related to the condition for which they were hospitalized. These infections result in about 90,000 deaths, and add between $4.5 to $5.7 billion per year to the costs of patient care.

Infections can also be a common complication of care in other settings including long term care facilities, clinics, and dialysis centers. Because recipients of care in other health care facilities are often transferred to and from hospital settings, the spread of infection is possible. Thus, infection prevention and control must be a priority in every setting.

Sharpening Standards Requirements

The Joint Commission's IC standards sharpen and raise expectations of organization leadership and of the infection control program itself. The IC standards emphasize how effective infection prevention and control requires an integrated, responsive process involving collaboration by many programs, services, and settings throughout the organization to develop, implement, and evaluate the IC program.

The standards underscore the importance of creating a plan to target the organization's surveillance activities, acting on the results of that surveillance and analyzing the efficacy of actions taken to prevent and control further infection. Individuals assigned responsibility for IC activities determine the scope and evaluate the efficacy of interventions. Strong organization leadership is needed to support infection prevention and control issues and allocate appropriate resources.

Infection control is an organizationwide issue. As such, it requires a commitment by organization leaders to not only make infection prevention and control a priority, but to provide the adequate resources for the appropriate interventions.

Reinforcing the Importance of Infection Control

Infection control issues are also addressed in standards in other chapters, such as "Management of the Environment of Care," "Management of Human Resources," "Improving Organization Performance," and "Leadership," to produce a comprehensive approach to infection control. The Joint Commission highlights the importance of effective infection control in several other ways as well, including the following:

- Making IC a focus for individual-based system and individual tracers

- Identifying compliance with the CDC's hand hygiene guidelines as a 2006 National Patient Safety Goal for all accredited organizations (*see* Chapter 2, pages 43–44)

- As a 2006 National Patient Safety Goal, requiring organizations to manage as sentinel events all death or major permanent loss of function identified that result from HAIs (*see* Chapter 2, pages 45–46)

- Advising accredited organizations that such HAIs should also be voluntarily reported to the Joint Commission's Sentinel Event database

Hand Hygiene

Infection control is problematic in almost any health care setting, and escalating rates of HAIs worry both patients and health care professionals.

If a caregiver is dealing with an infected or draining wound, the need for hand hygiene and gloving is obvious. However, normal, intact human skin is also colonized by bacteria—in differing amounts depending on the area of the body. This fact means that supposedly "clean" activities such as taking a pulse or blood pressure reading or lifting a patient can still result in caregivers acquiring a significant number of pathogens on their hands.[2]

The Joint Commission's IC standards focus on reducing the risks of HAIs and, in the case of hospitals, call for at least one activity in the infection control process to be aimed at preventing the transmission of infections between patients and staff. Infections that are common to all settings include catheter-associated urinary tract infections, bloodstream infections (usually associated with intravascular devices), and pneumonia. Ambulatory care and acute care providers also battle surgical-site infections, while home care and long term care professionals often deal with skin and soft tissue infections.[3–5]

Despite numerous interventions to increase health care workers' awareness of and compliance with good hand hygiene practices, compliance rates remain steady at only 25% to 50%.[2] Because the gap in time between not performing hand hygiene and the time when the patient gets an infection is days, staff do not often see the link; as a result, they do not get immediate feedback in time to respond. This problem can be especially true of staff in high-risk, high-volume areas of an organization, such as an emergency department or intensive care unit (ICU). The high-risk areas where hand hygiene is the most important are the areas where it may be the most neglected.

Hand hygiene is the most effective way to reduce infection transmission. CDC studies indicate that the new waterless hand sanitizer solutions are as effective as soap and water because the new solutions do not dry out hands. Dryness leads to skin cracks, which become reservoirs for pathogens, leading to infections among health care workers and transmission of infections to others. Other antimicrobial soaps have not been proven as beneficial because they can contribute to the antibiotic resistance problem.

The safety standards in the PC chapter describe involving the patient as a partner in the care process. Following this logic, organizations should teach patients to ask all caregivers whether they have washed their hands before they provide care. Through this approach, education can help reduce infection risk and enhance safety.

Surgical Site Infections

Postoperative surgical site infections (SSIs) are a major source of illness in both inpatients and outpatients, accounting for about one fourth of HAIs each year.[6] Preventive measures in all related settings can help avoid the longer hospitalizations or readmissions and higher costs associated with these infections. In 1999, the CDC issued a comprehensive guideline for SSI prevention that can be used by outpatient settings as well as hospitals. The following five areas summarize some of the CDC's recommendations:

- Preoperative Preparation of the Patient. Effective assessment of the patient is important because all infections remote from the surgical site should be identified and treated before a procedure is performed. If possible, elective procedures should be postponed until any infection has been resolved.

- Antimicrobial Prophylaxis. A prophylactic antimicrobial agent should be administered only when indicated and selected based on its efficacy against the most common pathogens associated with SSIs for a specific procedure.

- Asepsis and Surgical Technique. The importance of aseptic techniques is emphasized for procedures during which intravascular devices are placed, spinal or epidural anesthesia catheters are placed, and intravenous medications are dispensed or administered.

- Postoperative Incision Care. The CDC guidelines recommend protecting surgical sites with a sterile dressing for 24 to 48 hours after "an incision that has been closed primarily." When a dressing must be changed, hand hygiene and use of sterile technique are important. Given the ever-increasing number of outpatient procedures being performed, it may also be helpful to instruct patients and/or family members about proper care of incisions, symptoms of SSIs, and what symptoms they should report to a clinician.

- Surveillance. Postoperative/postdischarge surveillance is important to spot trends in types of infection, populations most affected, most problematic procedures, and so on. As with other kinds of data collection, common definitions are needed to ensure that comparisons are valid. Standardized definitions of SSIs can be used to identify infections for both inpatients (including readmissions) and outpatients, limiting interpretation about what constitutes an SSI to specified criteria.

Integrating Laboratory Concerns into a Patient Safety Program

As health care organizations evaluate processes for ways to reduce risks to patient safety, departments throughout each facility become involved. However, one area that is often overlooked is the in-house clinical laboratory. Although laboratory staff are not responsible for direct patient care, many laboratory-related processes, including dispensing blood and blood products as well as specimen collection, identification, and/or handling, can pose significant risks to patients if they are not performed correctly.

The laboratory plays a key role in improving patient safety. Many complex issues need to be addressed relative to patient safety and laboratory testing. Laboratory processes are no longer considered to be contained within the walls of an isolated department. Regulatory requirements and accreditation standards indicate that all activities from ordering to reporting and using test results are to be included. The conclusion of a study on mistakes in a stat laboratory is that "if patients' interests are to be safeguarded and quality in laboratory testing promoted, there must be a departure from the conventional view of the laboratory, which focuses on the quality control of the analytical activities within the laboratory. Today, the quality system for clinical laboratories must include promotion of accuracy in the analytical phase as well as the assurance of reliability of pre-and postanalytical activities. Our finding that a large percentage of laboratory mistakes occurs in the pre- and postanalytical phases indicates that the active monitoring of all potential defects calls for the assistance of nonlaboratory personnel to enable the inclusion of steps outside the laboratory."[7]

Everyone involved in any of the processes, including ordering tests, collecting and transporting specimens, testing specimens, reporting results, and those reacting to results, can affect patient outcomes or patient safety. In every step, there is the potential of adversely affecting the outcome. It might be a patient identification issue or that the wrong test is ordered, thereby delaying treatment until the right test is performed. In a sense, anyone involved in any of these steps is part of the laboratory and also part of the solution.

Another complicating factor is that some laboratory testing is now conducted outside the central laboratory in most health care organizations. Although point-of-care testing (POCT) has improved turnaround time and, in many cases, patient care, it also calls for new or adapted rules for assuring that reported results are correct. The processes for POCT are always better and therefore safer for patients when laboratory and testing staff can work together as a team with their combined expertise.

The Clinical Laboratory Improvement Amendments of 1988 (CLIA '88) have separated the various stages of laboratory testing to preanalytic, analytic, and post-analytic processes. This classification is helpful for defining where errors are most likely to occur in the laboratory testing processes.

Preanalytic Processes

Various studies have indicated that most errors associated with laboratory tests occur in the preanalytic phase. In a comprehensive literature search, the frequency of errors in this phase range from 32% to 75%.[8] The errors relate to the perceived need for a laboratory test, test requisition errors, inadequate patient preparation, and errors in specimen acquisition and processing. The wide range of errors for each category reflects the lack of consistent definitions regarding what constitutes a laboratory error.

The escalating increase in the numbers and variety of tests available have made communication about new methods or analytes a necessary part of laboratory services. To the extent that such consultation is available to clinicians, they are less likely to order tests inappropriately. Communication from the laboratory can also assist with reducing other error types in this phase. Laboratories are required to provide instructions for test requisition and patient preparation.

Some of the problems that can occur include the following:

- A test requisition system that is not user friendly; this might include problems with similar test names or abbreviations

- Inadequate patient preparation that could provide questionable patient results if the test is performed or that could require a delay in patient testing until the preparation is appropriate

■ There are a variety of ways to err with specimen collection and processing. Laboratories have traditionally provided and trained phlebotomy staff for collecting blood specimens. Although many continue to provide this service, there has been a move in some organizations for nursing to take over this function. Unless this transition takes place with full cooperation between the laboratory and nursing, a rise in error rates could occur. Issues include the following:

   • Proper patient identification and specimen labeling

   • The use of appropriate blood containers for the tests requested

   • Proper mixing of specimens that are anticoagulated

In addition to blood draws, other specimens collected by nonlaboratory staff include specimens for culture, cytology, and surgical pathology. If collected improperly, these specimens can also provide erroneous results and affect decisions about patient care in a number of ways, including turn-around-time for the result, not having the correct result for the right patient, or even delaying patient discharge.

Written procedures and guidelines for collection of all types of specimens for laboratory testing must be readily available to and used by staff collecting those specimens. In many organizations, these procedures are available online rather than in hard copy. Although this makes it easy for the laboratory to update procedures without having to update manuals in each patient care area, it also presents the challenge of making these procedures easily accessible. It is common for nursing staff to have difficulty accessing specimen collection procedures when asked. Also, an outdated procedure may still be used or multiple processes may exist in hard copy.

Analytic Processes

The testing process has been the focus of regulatory and accrediting bodies for a number of years. In addition, testing instruments and methodologies have become ever more reliable. Although errors do still occur in this phase, it is the least problematic of the three phases. Error frequency in the analytic process ranges between 4% and 32%. POCT has a higher error frequency than traditional laboratory settings.[8]

Quality control processes and review of patient results in the laboratory setting along with computerized flagging of results that vary from those the patient has had historically (delta checks) have helped to control errors in this phase. In addition, staff performing testing and review functions need to have a mindset of evaluating the data for results that do not make sense. There is no substitute for knowledge and judgment along with the willingness to repeat the testing process or even recollect a specimen, when it is indicated.

Postanalytic Processes

The postanalytic process includes reporting and interpretation of results. It is estimated that this phase gives rise to 9% to 55% of errors. The interpretation of results is an area where conscientious clinical consultation from the laboratory's pathologists is a vital support to the clinicians using the results.

Critical values that indicate a potentially life-threatening condition are a special problem. These values are to be immediately called to an individual who will understand the emergent situation signified by the result. As part of its National Patient Safety Goals, the Joint Commission has added a requirement for the laboratory staff member calling the result to obtain a read-back of the result (goal 2). However, there are other issues that need to be addressed in reporting critical values, such as the following:[9]

■ Calling the result to someone who can take action

■ Linking the patient at all times to a responsible physician

■ Documenting full information: patient name, test, value, date, time, reporter, and receiver

■ Requiring acknowledgement of receipt of the report

■ Having a clearly-understood backup system and avoiding a chain of reporting

- Using a central call system

- Agreeing on which test results require communication

- Using the same policy across all settings and domains

- This type of analysis for any process is preferable to assigning blame when the process is not working well.

Transfusion Errors

A special area where the laboratory interacts with those providing patient care and where the risk is great is that of blood transfusions. In several studies performed, the major source of error was misidentification. Included in this were absent wristbands; multiple wristbands; incomplete, erroneous, or illegible data; wrong wristbands; wrong blood tube being used; and wrong blood being transfused. The identification processes for all phases of specimen collection, testing, and blood transfusion have been defined and underscored in attempts to reduce errors. The high-risk nature of the blood transfusion process requires that all staff involved be educated and then periodically reminded about the necessity for clear identification of the patient, the specimens, and the unit of blood or blood product.

Some organizations periodically perform tracers on the identification process from taking the order to picking up the unit of blood and identifying the patient at the bedside. This can help keep the reasons for the structured requirements fresh in the minds of staff members, as well as help to identify places where it might be breaking down. One area where problems have been identified is float staff and contract staff who are not properly oriented or reoriented, as needed.

Beyond the Written Rules—Communication, Communication, Communication

Well thought out, clearly defined systems are important for patient safety. However, systems do not take the place of open interaction between physicians, nurses, and other clinicians who care for patients and the laboratory. Communication is essential to

quality patient care. The more these individuals can perceive themselves as belonging to the same team and less as adversaries, the better the chances of reducing errors. This can present quite a challenge in today's health care milieu where staffing in many organizations is at the bare minimum, but is absolutely necessary.

Areas where the laboratory and clinical staff need to work together include the following:

- Ongoing collaboration about blood bank and transfusion identification processes

- Education about new or existing laboratory tests, the indications for performing them, and the meaning of abnormal results

- The critical value list and processes to improve response to life-threatening values

- Proper specimen collection practices, including patient and specimen identification

- Ongoing collaboration for POCT

In addition, laboratory leaders should have some means of being readily available to physicians and nurses who have questions about testing processes or results. There needs to be an open attitude toward redefining processes that make sense to the laboratory, but do not work well for others who need to use the system.

By including laboratory staff in patient safety planning and evaluation activities, organizations can tap into an important source of information. Their expertise and compliance with Joint Commission requirements for trending data, addressing sentinel events, designing effective processes, and coordinating communication and other processes through department leaders mean they can contribute both knowledge and practical assistance in meeting organization-wide patient safety goals.

Staffing Effectiveness

Health care literature is full of studies that document the positive correlation between patient outcomes and proper staffing in health care organizations. In addition to contributing to a safe environment, appropriate staffing can also increase employee satisfaction. However, such staffing is by no means easy to achieve. In this era of staffing shortages, organization leaders can ensure that their staff members are meeting patient needs by monitoring staffing effectiveness.*

Staffing effectiveness involves more than simply the number of direct and indirect care providers working in a specific area. The Joint Commission defines staffing as the number, competency, and skill mix of staff relative to the provision of needed care, treatment, and services. Given current shortages of trained and experienced health care personnel, most organizations are struggling to define and attain an optimum level and mix of staff to ensure the provision of quality care. The task is difficult because many issues must be examined. When projecting staffing needs, managers should consider the following:

- The organization's mission

- The case mix of patients and the degree and complexity of care required

- The plan for the provision of patient care, treatment, and services

- The services provided by the organization

- The technology used in care, treatment, and services

- The expectations of the organization, the individuals it serves, and other customers

- Recruiting challenges, such as the difficulty of finding staff with particular expertise

- Financial resources

- Staffing plans by unit, program, or department

- Staffing variance reports

Through effective measurement and analysis, leaders can identify improvement opportunities and change processes to enhance patient safety. Strategies that

organizations might consider when addressing staffing effectiveness issues include the following:

- Develop staffing plans based on the level and scope of care, treatment, and services provided; the frequency of care, treatment, and services provided; and the level and competency of staff necessary to provide quality care, treatment, and services

- Monitor staffing level, mix, and competency to ensure the provision of safe, quality care that is satisfactory to both patients and staff

- Directly observe staffing levels to determine possible staffing inadequacies. Noncompliance with standards or organization policies and procedures often indicates staffing inadequacy.

- Cross-train staff to help ensure staffing adequacy. Cross-training staff creates an internal float pool that can be used during periods of peak census and high staff vacancy. Individualized cross-training meets the learning needs of each staff member and varies in length according to each individual's level of knowledge, experience, and skills.

- Proper staffing can help prevent errors that can lead to sentinel events. Following are some tips to help organizations reduce staffing adcquacy–related errors:

  - Determine staffing levels based on the number of patient care hours required to attain the best outcomes, not simply to care for patients

  - Track projected staffing needs against qualifications and competencies of current staff to identify any deficiencies. Improve staffing levels as needed.

  - Stay alert to staffing adequacy during holidays, off-shifts, and following a dramatic census increase. Adjust staffing as treatment modalities and criteria for discharge are altered.

  - Adjust staffing numbers to allocate for the necessary number of clinical staff to provide care, treatment, and services and to frequently assess the patient in restraint or seclusion.

---

* The Joint Commission's staffing effectiveness standards currently apply only to hospitals and long term care organizations.

Ensure that psychiatric and/or behavioral units have adequate numbers of staff to quickly, effectively, and safely apply restraint or help the individual into a seclusion area.

- Provide timely job-specific, safety-related orientation and training for all staff, particularly float and agency staff

- Focus on staff education and develop and implement effective recruitment and retention strategies

The Staffing Standards

The assessment of staffing effectiveness is one of the most controversial issues debated about health care quality today. Discussions of staff-to-patient ratios abound within state legislatures, with some stepping in to mandate specific ratios in specific settings. However, the authors of an Institute of Medicine report on nursing staff adequacy in hospitals and long term care facilities rejected the idea of mandatory minimum staffing levels.[10]

The Joint Commission's staffing-related standards require organization leaders and staff to consider data from clinical/service screening indicators (for example, patient or resident falls or adverse drug reactions) independently and in combination with human resources indicators (for example, staff overtime and vacancy rates), to identify any possible staffing needs and to assess staffing effectiveness. This requirement should not cause new work for organizations as most already collect these data.

To comply with the staffing standards, organizations should identify indicators from a list provided by the Joint Commission, as well as their own indicators, if they choose to do so (*see* Sidebar 4-3, "Joint Commission-Approved Subjects for Screening Indicators for Hospitals and Long Term Care Organizations," on pages 135–136). Processes known to jeopardize patient safety should be measured. Because no single indicator tells the whole story, each organization should track a matrix of staffing-related indicators unique to its own issues and environment. This model for assessing staffing effectiveness recommended by the Joint Commission provides much more flexibility than the ratio approach under discussion in various legislatures.

The staffing standard requires health care organizations to collect data on relevant human resource and clinical/service screening indicators for a minimum of two units/divisions* (populations/settings† for long term care), determine the desired performance for each indicator, trend the data over time, and analyze variation from desired performance. It may be appropriate to rotate the units/divisions (populations/settings for long term care) being monitored over time after sufficient data have been reviewed to conclude that care on these units is stable. The use of multiple indicators increases the likelihood that existing problems will be identified and appropriately characterized. The use of nursing-sensitive measures makes it likely that problems identified will be staffing-related. However, this will not be universally true— the types of root causes may be identified and will need to be addressed.

How to Use the Staffing Standards

Hospitals and long term care organizations surveyed by the Joint Commission are required to comply with the staffing standards that address assessing staffing effectiveness. Organization staff can comply with the standards by following this eight-step process:

1. Review standards. Organizations should carefully review the standards and elements of performance (EPs) in all areas where staffing needs are being planned.

2. Select appropriate screening indicators. Leaders should review the revised standards and the list of screening indicators and ask themselves, "What indicators are relevant to the departments or units being served?" Information from safety, PI, risk management, and other sources should be considered in determining indicators.

Organizations must select a minimum of four indicators for each identified inpatient units/divisions (populations/settings for

---

* Unit/division refers to level at which staffing is planned and is provided within the organization. For example, staffing may be planned for individual units or for a group of units, such as all medical/surgical units.

† Populations/settings refers to level in which staffing is planned and is provided within the organization. For example, staffing may be provided for individual populations or settings or may be planned for a group of settings or populations.

Sidebar 4-3. Joint Commission-Approved Subjects for Screening Indicators for Hospitals and Long Term Care Organizations

For Hospitals

Clinical/Service Indicators

1. Patient/Family complaints/satisfaction
2. Adverse drug events
3. Injuries to patients
4. Skin breakdown
5. Pneumonia
6. Postoperative infections
7. Urinary tract infections
8. Upper gastrointestinal bleeding
9. Shock/cardiac arrest
10. Length of stay
11. Death among surgical inpatients with treatable serious complications (failure to rescue) (National Quality Forum measure)
12. Pressure ulcer prevalence (National Quality Forum measure)
13. Falls prevalence (National Quality Forum measure)
14. Falls with injury (National Quality Forum measure)
15. Restraint prevalence (vest and limb only) (National Quality Forum measure)
16. Urinary catheter-associated urinary tract infection for intensive care unit patients (National Quality Forum measure)
17. Central line catheter-associated blood stream infection rate for intensive care unit and high-risk nursery patients (National Quality Forum measure)
18. Ventilator-associated pneumonia for intensive care unit and high-risk nursery patients (National Quality Forum measure)
19. Smoking cessation counseling for acute myocardial infarction (National Quality Forum measure)
20. Smoking cessation counseling for heart failure (National Quality Forum measure)
21. Smoking cessation counseling for pneumonia (National Quality Forum measure)

Human Resources Indicators

22. Overtime
23. Staff vacancy rate
24. Staff satisfaction
25. Staff turnover rate
26. Understaffing as compared to organization's staffing plan
27. Staff injuries on the job
28. On-call or per diem use
29. Sick time
30. Agency staff use
31. Skill mix (registered nurse, licensed vocational nurse/licensed practical nurse, unlicensed assistive personnel, and contract) (National Quality Forum measure)
32. Nursing care hours per patient day (registered nurse, licensed practical nurse, and unlicensed assistive personnel) (National Quality Forum measure)

33. Practice Environment Scale-Nursing Work Index (PES-NWI) composite and five subscales (National Quality Forum measure)
34. Voluntary turnover (National Quality Forum measure)

For Long Term Care

Clinical/Service Indicators

1. Prevalence of pressure ulcers
2. Resident satisfaction
3. Family satisfaction
4. Prevalence of falls
5. Resident complaints
6. Injuries to residents
7. Family complaints
8. Restraint use
9. Prevalence of unintended weight loss
10. Elopements/wandering of residents
11. Adverse drug events
12. Prevalence of dehydration
13. Pain assessment and management (that is, wait time to receive medications)
14. Urinary tract infection rate
15. Change in resident functioning
16. Prevalence of malnutrition
17. Activities of daily living (ADLs) met or unmet
18. Prevalence of urinary catheter use
19. Average time in activities
20. Antibiotic use
21. Unexpected hospital admissions or emergency department visits
22. Prevalence of untreated depression
23. Prevalence of more than eight prescribed medications
24. Pneumonia rate
25. Unnecessary antipsychotic medication usage

Chronic Care Measures

26. Residents whose need for more help with daily activities has increased (National Quality Forum Measure)
27. Residents who lost too much weight (National Quality Forum Measure)
28. Residents who experience moderate to severe pain during the seven-day assessment period (Clinical/Service) (National Quality Forum Measure)
29. Residents who were physically restrained during the seven-day assessment period (National Quality Forum Measure)

(continued)

Sidebar 4-3. *(continued)*

30. Residents who spent most of their time in bed or in a chair in their room during the seven-day assessment period (National Quality Forum Measure)

31. Residents with a decline in their ability to move about in their room or the adjacent corridor (National Quality Forum Measure)

32. Residents with a urinary tract infection (National Quality Forum Measure)

33. Residents with worsening of a depressed or anxious mood (National Quality Forum Measure)

Chronic Care Measure Pairs

34. High-risk residents with pressure ulcers *and* average-risk residents with pressure ulcers (National Quality Forum Measure)

35. Residents who frequently lose control of the bowel or bladder (low-risk) *and* residents who have a catheter in the bladder at any time during the 14-day assessment period (National Quality Forum Measure)

Postacute Care Measures

36. Recently hospitalized residents with symptoms of delirium (National Quality Forum Measure)

37. Recently hospitalized residents who experienced moderate to severe pain at any time during the seven-day assessment period (National Quality Forum Measure)

38. Recently hospitalized residents with pressure ulcers (National Quality Forum Measure)

Measures for All Nursing Home Residents

39. Pneumococcal polysaccharide vaccination of residents age 65 or older (National Quality Forum Measure)

40. Influenza vaccination for all nursing home residents (National Quality Forum Measure)

Human Resources Indicators

41. Staff vacancy rate

42. Staff turnover rate

43. Staff satisfaction

44. Use of overtime

45. Staff injury rate

46. Nursing hours per resident day (registered nurse, licensed practical nurse, certified nursing assistant) compared to baseline such as actual versus planned or budgeted

47. Staff training hours

48. Agency usage/contract staff

49. Understaffing as compared to organization's staffing plan

50. Use of sick time

51. Activity staff hours per resident day

52. Number of dietary staff hours per resident day

53. Number of housekeeping staff hours per resident day

54. Average response time for consultation order

55. Nurse staffing hours (National Quality Forum Measure)

Note: *Additional information on nursing home care measures can be found at http://www.qualityforum.org.*

---

long term care). Organizations determine the indicators for each unit/division (populations/settings for long term care) based on assessment of relevant information or risk, including the following:

■ Knowledge about staffing issues likely to impact patient/resident safety or quality of care

■ Patient/resident population served

■ Type of setting

■ Review of existing data (for example, incident logs, sentinel event data, performance improvement reports)

■ Input from clinical staff who provide patient/resident care

The four indicators chosen for each inpatient unit/division (population/setting for long term care) must include two clinical/service indicators and two human resources indicators; one of the clinical/service indicators and one of the human resources indicators must be selected from the Joint Commission's list of approved screening indicators (*see* Sidebar 4-3 on pages 135–136). The organization may select additional indicators from among its own indicators, such as those that might be drawn from risk management data, incident reports, patient survey questionnaires, and other human resources data. All nursing staff (including registered nurses, licensed practical nurses, and nursing assistants or aides) are included in the human resource indicators for all identified units/divisions (populations/settings for long term care).

Note: *Decisions regarding stratification of data by discipline are left to the organization.*

It is helpful to have an interdisciplinary team select the indicators. The staff needs to be educated about the requirements and understand that staffing effectiveness is not just a nursing concept but a priority for the organization.

3. Collect data from a minimum of two Units/Departments. Retrospective data can be used, as should data identified from the selected screening indicators. Leaders should specify a minimum data collection period and data should be sufficient to yield statistically significant information. An organization may wish to appoint a "champion" in the organization who takes responsibility for accurate and timely data collection.

4. Aggregate and display data. PI tools should be used to summarize data. Individual indicator analysis can be facilitated through the use of line graphs, run charts, control charts, and other display tools. Staff should perform historical trending for each indicator. Aggregate indicator analysis should combine information that pertains to the set of selected screening indicators.

5. Analyze indicators individually and compare them to one another. Staff should ask, "What impact, if any, did staffing (number, skill mix, and competency) have on the outcomes?" "Is the variation seen in individual indicators the result of common or special causes?" "Are similar trends seen across multiple indicators for the same time period or periods?" "Can similar causes be established, linking some of the indicators?" Cause-and-effect diagrams, process flowcharts, brainstorming, and other PI tools can help identify root causes that require PI initiatives. Staff can also ask, "Where and at what times are incidents occurring?" For example, are they occurring only on weekends or on off-shifts? Is one department having more incidents than others? If so, interdepartmental collaboration and the sharing of lessons learned can be effective in reducing the incidence of adverse occurrences.

6. Identify opportunities for improvements. Indicators that fall within suboptimal ranges should be targeted for improvement initiatives. Or, at the very least, changes pertaining to staffing effectiveness (such as number of staff, skill mix, and staff competence) may need to be made. For example, staff at one organization completed a statistical study that indicated a positive correlation between the postoperative pneumonia rate and RN vacancy rate on its surgical units. Staff asked, "How could the vacancy rate be improved to reduce the incidence of postoperative pneumonia? What other solutions could improve this situation?"

7. Use Plan, Do, Check, and Act or another PI methodology to improve staffing effectiveness. Brainstorm and/or consult the professional literature to identify potential staffing effectiveness strategies, such as enhanced staff recruitment, increased education and training, service reduction, equipment enhancements, reorganization of work flow, and other strategies.

8. Reevaluate screening indicators for relevancy and sensitivity for the unit. Individual indicators and the overall mix of screening indicators may need to be modified from time to time.

Making It Happen

Leadership buy-in provides the start. The entire staff—including nursing, physical and occupational therapy, nutrition, and housekeeping—needs to be educated about the requirements and to under-stand that staffing effectiveness is not just a nursing concept but a priority for the organization. Interdisciplinary teams should select the indicators. It might also help to identify a "champion" in the organization who wishes to be responsible for accurate and timely data collection. A "champion" does not have to be someone who knows how to analyze or graph the data, but someone who can ensure consistency and integrity of data collection.

The staffing effectiveness requirements challenge organizations to evaluate what the numbers mean and whether they relate to one another. Doing so will help organizations solve ongoing problems that could affect patient and resident safety.

References

1. American Association of Suicidology: U.S.A. Suicide: 2002 Official Final Data. (accessed Jan. 6, 2006 at http://www.suicidology.org/associations/1045/files/2002FinalData.pdf).

2. Boyce J.M., Pittet D.: *Guideline for Hand Hygiene in Health-Care Settings. Recommendations of the Healthcare Infection Control Practices Advisory Committee and the HICPAC/SHEA/ APIC/IDSA Hand Hygiene Task Force.* #51(RR16). Atlanta: Centers for Disease Control and Prevention, Oct. 25, 2002. Available at http://www.cdc.gov/handhygiene.

3. Burke J.P.: Infection control—A problem for patient safety. *N Engl J Med* 348:651–656, Feb. 13, 2003.

4. Nicolle L.E.: Preventing infections in non-hospital settings: Long-term care. *Emerg Infect Dis* 7:205–207, Mar.–Apr. 2001.

5. Rhinehart E.: Infection control in home care. *Emerg Infect Dis* 7:208–211, Mar.–Apr. 2001.

6. Nichols R.L.: Preventing surgical site infections: A surgeon's perspective. *Emerging Infectious Diseases.* Mar.–Apr. 2001. http://www.cdc.gov/ncidod/eid/vol7no2/nichols.htm.

7. Plebani, M., Carraro, P.: Mistakes in a stat laboratory: types and frequency. *Clin Chem* 43:8; 1348–1351, 1997.

8. Bonini P., Plebani M., Ceriotti F., Rubboli F.: Errors in Laboratory Medicine. *Clin Chem* 48:5; 691–698, 2002.

9. Leape L.L.: Beyond the Quality Institute Conference 2003. *Patient Safety, The New Accountability.*

10. Wunderlich G.D., Sloan F.A., Davis C.K.: *Nursing staff in hospitals and nursing homes: Is it adequate?* Report from the Institute of Medicine's Committee on the Adequacy of Nurse Staffing in Hospitals and Nursing Homes. Washington, D.C.: National Academy Press, 1996, pp. 121–122.

CHAPTER 5

Addressing Patient Safety in the Joint Commission's Accreditation Process

While health care organizations differ in size, scope, and clinical care, they do share a common dedication to provide safe and high-quality care, treatment, and services to the individuals they serve. Because of this, organizations strive to continuously improve their services and processes in response to the changing needs of the populations they serve and to the changing health care environment.

The Joint Commission is also dedicated to improving its services to better support the quality and safety efforts of health care organizations. As such, the Joint Commission's accreditation process shifts the organization's focus from survey preparation to ongoing improvement and clarifies the relationship between the standards and how processes function within a health care organization.

This chapter provides a discussion of the various components of the accreditation process, including the following:

- Periodic Performance Review

- Priority Focus Process

- Onsite survey process

- Decision process

While the discussion will offer a brief description of each component, special attention will be paid to the role safety plays in the accreditation process. In addition, this chapter will discuss the move to unannounced surveys, effective January 2006.

Periodic Performance Review

The Periodic Performance Review (PPR) allows organizations to continuously comply with Joint Commission standards through an ongoing, systematic approach to maintaining

safe, quality care, treatment, and services. Accredited organizations can use the PPR process to assess and attest to (or have assessed for them) compliance with all applicable standards and Accreditation Participation Requirements (APRs). Ambulatory care, behavioral health care, home care, hospitals, laboratories, and long term care organizations are required to participate in the PPR. Critical access hospitals and office-based surgery practices may be added in the future.

Because the PPR is a full evaluation of standards, it makes the accreditation process more continuous. The PPR provides a tool for leadership to identify the areas in which an organization should invest time and resources for improvements. Undergoing a thorough standards review facilitates an organization's efforts to incorporate the concepts within the standards into routine operations. This incorporation improves the safety and quality of care, treatment, and services.

Priority Focus Process

The Priority Focus Process (PFP) uses information about an individual health care organization to more clearly focus the organization's PPR and its on-site survey on areas most important to its provision of safe, quality care. The PFP gathers data from multiple sources and analyzes it consistently across all health care organizations using a set of defined and automated rules, thus turning data into information. The PFP tool reviews presurvey materials. PFP data are available for ambulatory care, behavioral health care, home care, hospital, laboratories, and long term care organizations.

Data Used

The information used in the PFP includes data the Joint Commission currently gathers, data from outside organizations such as

Centers for Medicare & Medicaid Services (CMS; for hospitals only), and health care organization data such as prior accreditation history and recommendations, ORYX data (for hospitals only), Office of Quality Monitoring data, and applicable performance measurement data.

The PFP integrates these various presurvey data and recommends priority focus areas (PFAs). These PFAs are processes, systems, or structures in a health care organization that can significantly impact the provision of safe, high-quality care; when performed well, these areas can lead to enhanced safety and high-quality care. A list of the 14 possible PFAs identified within the PFP, along with their definitions, is shown in Sidebar 5-1 on pages 141–143. (These categories may change slightly in the future as more information is gleaned through the accreditation process.) During an on-site survey, surveyors link these PFAs with standards compliance issues to identify potential underlying vulnerabilities.

Two weeks before a full survey, the Joint Commission makes PFP information available to an organization and surveyors who will be surveying the organization. This summary gives the surveyor time to become familiar with the organization, the services it provides, and organization-specific issues that are most relevant in assessing safety and quality of care.

The PFP summary includes the following:

- Demographic information

- The top four specific PFAs for that organization. If several areas seem to have similar priority needs, the organization's list of PFAs or clinical/service groups (CSGs) could be longer than the four generally provided to health care organizations.

- The top CSGs for the organization. CSGs are groups of patients in distinct, clinical populations for which data are collected. Tracer patients are selected according to CSGs.

- Standards associated with the PFAs

With enhanced insight and information about each organization before survey, surveyors can finalize plans for survey activities. This process allows the Joint

Commission to customize accreditation to individual health care organizations by focusing survey activities on organization-specific issues that may be most relevant to improving safety and quality of care. Having CSGs and PFAs identified for the particular organization, surveyors can choose individuals for initial tracers using a consistent rationale and then trace the chosen individuals in a focused manner. (Based on survey findings, surveyors might select individuals for tracers who are not identified by PFP.) Refer to pages 143–145 in this chapter for more detail on tracer methodology.

For example, consider a hospital that reports ORYX core measure data for heart failure patients. Based on these and other data, the PFP prioritizes cardiac patients as one of the CSGs to be traced, and it identifies Communication, Assessment, Medication Use, and Quality Improvement Expertise and Activity as PFAs. For a tracer activity, the surveyor selects a heart failure patient who was admitted through the emergency department and is still an active inpatient.

The PFP summary provides a health care organization with additional information about the processes, systems, and structures within the organization that might impact the safety and quality of care provided. That summary, in turn, initiates an organization-specific evaluation process. The PFP helps direct a prioritized on-site assessment of an organization's systems. Surveyors perform individual and system tracer activities and evaluate standards compliance. Regardless of an organization's PFP information, a surveyor will assess the organization's compliance with any standards issues that are raised as he or she conducts the survey.

Because initial tracer activities are selected according to CSGs identified in the PFP and might initially focus on the PFAs, related accreditation standards, and other issues that arise during the on-site survey, the result is an accreditation process that is closely tailored to what affects each organization's safety and quality of care.

An organization is not restricted in applying information gained from the PFP only at the time of survey or midway through the accreditation cycle when it completes its PPR. Health care organizations can use information about all PFAs to continuously

Sidebar 5-1. The Joint Commission's Priority Focus Areas

Assessment and Care/Services Assessment and Care/Services for patients comprise the execution of a series of processes including, as relevant: assessment; planning care, treatment, and/or services; provision of care; ongoing reassessment of care; and discharge planning, referral for continuing care, or discontinuation of services. Assessment and Care/Services are fluid in nature to accommodate a patient's needs while in a care setting. While some elements of Assessment and Care/Services may occur only once, other aspects may be repeated or revisited as the patient's needs or care delivery priorities change. Successful implementation of improvements in Assessment and Care/Services rely on the full support of leadership.

Subprocesses of Assessment and Care/Services include the following:

- Assessment

- Reassessment

- Planning care, treatment, and services

- Provision of care, treatment, and services

- Discharge planning or discontinuation of services

Communication Communication is the process by which information is exchanged between individuals, departments, or organizations. Effective communication successfully permeates every aspect of a health care organization, from the provision of care to performance improvement, resulting in a marked improvement in the quality of care delivery and functioning.

Subprocesses of Communication include the following:

- Provider and/or staff-patient communication

- Patient and family education

- Staff communication and collaboration

- Information dissemination

- Multidisciplinary teamwork

Credentialed Practitioners Credentialed Practitioners are health care professionals whose qualifications to provide patient care services have been verified and assessed, resulting in the granting of clinical privileges. They typically are not employed staff at the health care organization. The category varies from organization to organization and from state to state. It includes licensed independent practitioners and, in some settings, nurse practitioners, advanced practice registered nurses, and physician assistants who are permitted to provide patient care services under the direction of a sponsoring physician. Licensed independent practitioners are permitted by law and the health care organization to provide care and services without clinical supervision or direction within the scope of their license and consistent with individually granted clinical privileges.

Equipment Use Equipment Use incorporates the selection, delivery, setup, and maintenance of equipment and supplies to meet patient and staff needs. It generally includes movable equipment, as well as management of supplies that staff members use (for example, gloves, syringes). (Equipment Use does not include fixed equipment such as built-in oxygen and gas lines and central air conditioning systems; this is included in the Physical Environment focus area.) Equipment Use includes planning and selecting; maintaining, testing, and inspecting; educating and providing instructions; delivery and setup; and risk prevention related to equipment and/or supplies.

Subprocesses of Equipment Use include the following:

- Selection

- Maintenance strategies

- Periodic evaluation

- Orientation and training

Infection Control Infection Control includes the surveillance/identification, prevention, and control of infections among patients, employees, physicians, and other licensed independent practitioners, contract service workers, volunteers, students, and visitors. This is a systemwide, integrated process that is applied to all programs, services, and settings.

Subprocesses of Infection Control include the following:

- Surveillance/identification

- Prevention and control

- Reporting

- Measurement

Information Management Information Management is the interdisciplinary field concerning the timely and accurate creation, collection, storage, retrieval, transmission, analysis, control, dissemination, and use of data or information, both within an organization and externally, as allowed by law and regulation. In addition to written and verbal information, supporting information technology and information services are also included in Information Management.

Subprocesses of Information Management include the following:

- Planning

- Procurement

- Implementation

- Collection

- Recording

- Protection

- Aggregation

- Interpretation

- Storage and retrieval

- Data integrity

- Information dissemination

Medication Management Medication Management encompasses the systems and processes an organization uses to provide medication to individuals served by the organization. This is

(continued)

Sidebar 5-1. *(continued)*

usually a multidisciplinary, coordinated effort of health care staff, implementing, evaluating, and constantly improving the processes of selecting, procuring, storing, ordering, transcribing, preparing, dispensing, administering (including self-administering), and monitoring the effects of medications throughout the patients' continuum of care. In addition, Medication Management involves educating patients and, as appropriate, their families, about the medication, its administration and use, and potential side effects.

Subprocesses of Medication Management include the following:

- Selection
- Procurement
- Storage
- Prescribing or ordering
- Preparing
- Dispensing
- Administration
- Monitoring

Organizational Structure The Organizational Structure is the framework for an organization to carry out its vision and mission. The implementation is accomplished through corporate bylaws and governing body policies, organization management, compliance, planning, integration and coordination, and performance improvement. Included are the organization's governance; business ethics, contracted organizations, and management requirements.

Subprocesses of Organizational Structure include the following:

- Management requirements
- Corporate by-laws and governing body plans
- Organization management
- Compliance
- Planning
- Business ethics
- Contracted services

Orientation & Training Orientation is the process of educating newly hired staff in health care organizations to organizationwide, departmental, and job-specific competencies before they provide patient care services. "Newly hired staff" includes, but is not limited to, regular staff employees, contracted staff, agency (temporary) staff, float staff, volunteer staff, students, housekeeping, and maintenance staff.

Training refers to the development and implementation of programs that foster staff development and continued learning, address skill deficiencies, and thereby help to ensure staff retention. More specifically, it entails providing opportunities for staff to develop enhanced skills related to revised processes that may have been addressed during orientation, new patient care techniques, or expanded job responsibilities. Whereas orientation is a one-time process, training is a continuous one.

Subprocesses of Orientation & Training include the following:

- Organizationwide orientation
- Departmental orientation
- Job-specific orientation
- Training and continuing or ongoing education

Patient Safety Effective Patient Safety entails proactively identifying the potential and actual risks to safety, identifying the underlying cause(s) of the potential, and making the necessary improvements so risk is reduced. It also entails establishing processes to respond to sentinel events, identifying cause through root cause analysis, and making necessary improvements. This involves a systems-based approach that examines all activities within an organization that contribute to the maintenance and improvement of patient safety, such as performance improvement and risk management to ensure the activities work together, not independently, to improve care and safety. The systems-based approach is driven by organization leadership, anchored in the organization's mission, vision, and strategic plan, endorsed and actively supported by medical staff and nursing leadership, implemented by directors, integrated and coordinated throughout the organization's staff, and continuously re-engineered using proven, proactive performance improvement modalities. In addition, effective reduction of errors and other factors that contribute to unintended adverse outcomes in an organization requires an environment in which patients, their families, and organization staff and leaders can identify and manage actual and potential risks to safety.

Subprocesses of Patient Safety include the following:

- Planning and designing services
- Directing services
- Integrating and coordinating services
- Error reduction and prevention
- The use of Sentinel Event Alerts
- Joint Commission's National Patient Safety Goals
- Clinical practice guidelines
- Active patient involvement in their care

Physical Environment The Physical Environment refers to safe, accessible, functional, supportive, and effective Physical Environment for patients, staff members, workers, and other individuals, by managing physical design; construction and redesign; maintenance and testing; planning and improvement; and risk prevention, defined in terms of utilities, fire protection, security, privacy, storage, and hazardous materials and waste. The Physical Environment may include the home in the case of home care and foster care.

Subprocesses of Physical Environment include the following:

- Physical design
- Construction and redesign
- Maintenance and testing
- Planning and improvement
- Risk prevention

(continued)

Sidebar 5-1. *(continued)*

Quality Improvement Expertise/Activities Quality Improvement identifies the collaborative and interdisciplinary approach to the continuous study and improvement of the processes of providing health care services to meet the needs of consumers and others. Quality Improvement depends on understanding and revising processes on the basis of data and knowledge about the processes themselves. Quality Improvement involves identifying, measuring, implementing, monitoring, analyzing, planning, and maintaining processes to ensure they function effectively. Examples of Quality Improvement Activities include designing a new service, flowcharting a clinical process, collecting and analyzing data about performance measures or patient outcomes, comparing the organization's performance to that of other organizations, selecting areas for priority attention, and experimenting with new ways of carrying out a function.

Subprocesses of Quality Improvement Expertise/Activities include the following:

- Identifying issues and establishing priorities
- Developing measures
- Collecting data to evaluate status on outcomes, processes, or structures
- Analyzing and interpreting data
- Making and implementing recommendations
- Monitoring and sustaining performance improvement

Rights & Ethics Rights & Ethics include patient rights and organizational ethics as they pertain to patient care. Rights & Ethics addresses issues such as patient privacy, confidentiality

and protection of health information, advance directives (as appropriate), organ procurement, use of restraints, informed consent for various procedures, and the right to participate in care decisions.

Subprocesses of Rights & Ethics include the following:

- Patient rights
- Organizational ethics pertaining to patient care
- Organizational responsibility
- Consideration of patient
- Care sensitivity
- Informing patients and/or family

Staffing Effective Staffing entails providing the optimal number of competent personnel with the appropriate skill mix to meet the needs of a health care organization's patients based on that organization's mission, values, and vision. As such, it involves defining competencies and expectations for all staff (the competency of licensed independent practitioners and medical staff are addressed in the Credentialed Practitioners priority focus area for all accreditation programs); Staffing includes assessing those defined competencies and allocating human resources necessary for patient safety and improved patient outcomes.

Subprocesses of Staffing include the following:

- Competency
- Skill mix
- Number of staff

---

assess their own essential processes. In doing so, they can identify ways to enhance the provision of quality patient care in their organization.

The On-Site Survey Process

A completely redesigned on-site survey process intended to be more relevant, patient-focused, and customized to each health care organization is a key component of the Joint Commission's accreditation process. The accreditation process changes the basic framework of how a surveyor assesses compliance with standards. Individual tracers—that is, following the care, treatment, and services provided to actual individuals—represent a patient-focused approach to evaluating standards compliance. The survey process has several goals including the following:

- Incorporate the tracer methodology and focus the survey on areas that are most

critical to the health care organization that is successfully providing safe, quality care

- Allow more time for education on high-priority issues

- Better engage direct care providers in the accreditation process

Using Tracer Methodology to Customize the Survey Process

Individual tracer activities allow surveyors to analyze how the organization provides care. Through this methodology, surveyors follow the course of care, treatment, and services as experienced by individual patients. They interact with the direct care providers in each area experienced by the patient and address the following:

- The relationships among disciplines/departments involved in care

- Integration and coordination of important processes

- Opportunities for improvement

- Education, as appropriate

Selecting Tracers

Surveyors use presurvey data gathered and interpreted through the PFP and other criteria to select patients for the individual tracer process. When a Joint Commission surveyor(s) arrives on site, he or she will request a list of active patients that includes the patients' names, current locations in the organization, and diagnoses (including 23-hour observation patients). The surveyor will then select initial charts based on the organization's CSGs.

The number of tracers conducted will depend on the size of the organization, the number of surveyors, and the length of the survey. It is estimated that 50% to 60% of each surveyor's time on site will be spent conducting tracers. Each surveyor individually engages in several tracers per survey. Because surveyors will be selecting multiple tracer patients, surveyors will make an effort to avoid selecting tracers that may overlap sites or staff within the organization.

Conducting the Tracer

An organization's top four PFAs identified in its PFP will guide the surveyor in conducting the tracer activities. After reviewing a tracer patient's medical record to identify units, sites, or departments that served the particular individual, the surveyor will begin to trace the care provided, even if that care is provided in a single room or in a home setting. As the surveyor conducts the tracer, he or she will observe direct patient care, medication processes, and care planning processes, or he or she will interview the individual and/or family, as appropriate, to discuss the course of care and to verify issues identified during the tracer. He or she will also observe environment of care and safety- and infection-control–related issues.

The surveyor will trace the entire care process from entry or admission through postdischarge. There is no set order in which surveyors will visit an organization's departments or areas. However, in order to review the patient record, surveyors will likely start where the patient is currently located and may sequentially follow the patient from where he or she first entered the organization to where he or she now is, or they may start in the unit more likely to contain issues that need assessment. While conducting a tracer activity, surveyors leave the clinical record in the patient care unit. The surveyor gathers enough information from reading the chart to describe the patient and treatment as the path is followed through the organization. The record stays where it is, available for ongoing reference and documentation by caregivers.

During the individual tracer process, the surveyor may at any time ask to review organization policies or procedures about the care provided to the patient if it becomes necessary or relevant to the discussion. Surveyors will note specific human resources or credentials files that they would like to review and will identify which equipment maintenance logs to check.

As surveyors move around a health care organization, they will ask to speak with the staff members who actually provided care to the patient being traced. If a specific staff member is not available, the surveyor will ask to speak to another staff member who would perform the same functions. During these discussions, the surveyor is focusing on how the care processes work.

The surveyor may also wish to speak with nonclinical support staff, such as housekeeping or food service, about infection control concerns, issues related to patient safety, or other matters relevant to the patient's care.

Each tracer can take anywhere from one to three hours to complete, depending on the complexity of the care provided to the patient, and may not be completed in a single session. Depending on how accessible records, staff, and even patients are, the surveyor may need to break up the time spent following the care of an individual patient. Because of the comprehensive nature of tracer activities, a surveyor could theoretically visit any location in the organization if it is related to the care provided to the tracer patient.

If the surveyor identifies a standards issue while tracing a patient, he or she might pull other records, active or closed, of similar patients to determine if the problem represents an isolated issue or a pattern. Based on the issue being evaluated, surveyors might request additional records with criteria of same or similar diagnosis as the original tracer patient, same age or sex as the original tracer patient, similar lengths of stay, or individuals close to discharge.

As multiple cases are examined throughout their actual care process, the surveyor may identify performance issue trends in one or more of the processes. The surveyor will then work with the organization to address these trends, offer ideas on ways to improve, share good practices from other health care organizations that are addressing the same issue, and provide guidance as needed. In addition, the surveyor may issue a requirement for improvement to the organization. The organization would then have 45 days to submit an Evidence of Standards Compliance (ESC) report and an indicator or a measure of success (MOS) that it will use to assess sustained compliance over time.

While tracer activities are generally conducted similarly across health care settings, the types of individuals who might be traced, the care elements to be traced, and the questions that would be generated based on the care, treatment, and services they receive change from setting to setting. Sidebar 5-2 on pages 146–154 illustrates how surveyors might use tracer methodology to follow an organization's processes of care. Actual tracers will differ from these examples.

Individual-based System Tracers. During the survey, surveyors also conduct individual-based system tracer activities focusing on important processes or functions that cut across an organization. These individual-based system tracers provide insight into the performance of an organization's functions or processes, specifically addressing the following:

■ The flow of a process across the organization, including identification of risk points and how they are managed; integration of key activities; and communication/coordination among staff/units involved in the process

■ Strengths and areas of concern as well as actions that could be taken in areas needing improvement

■ Issues requiring further exploration in subsequent survey activities

■ Baseline assessment of standards compliance

■ Education, as appropriate

During individual-based system tracers, surveyors may facilitate discussions and encourage the organization staff to identify opportunities for improvement. Like individual tracers, individual-based system tracers may also include visits to departments or areas directly involved in the process under discussion.

The three topics evaluated through individual-based system tracers are data use, infection control, and medication management:

■ Data Use: The data use individual-based system tracer focuses on how the organization collects, analyzes, interprets, and uses data to improve patient safety and care.

■ Infection Control: The infection control individual-based system tracer explores the organization's infection control processes. The goals of this session are to assess the organization's compliance with the relevant infection control standards, identify infection control issues that require further exploration, and determine actions that may be necessary to address any identified risks and improve patient safety.

■ Medication Management: The medication management individual-based system tracer explores the organization's medication management processes, while focusing on subprocesses and potential risk points (such as hand-off points). This tracer activity helps the surveyors evaluate the continuity of medication management from procurement of medications through the monitoring of their effects on patients.

The data use individual-based system tracer is conducted on all surveys; during surveys of fewer than three days, there may not be time for separate medication management and infection control tracers. In such cases, these two topics are evaluated as part of the data use individual-based system tracer and individual tracers.

Sidebar 5-2.
Sample Tracers

The following are fictional examples of individual tracers that could take place in a variety of health care settings (ambulatory care, behavioral health care, home care, hospice, hospital, and long term care). The questions contained with each example represent only a sampling of the kinds of areas that a surveyor may explore during a tracer.

Individual Tracer Example: Ambulatory Care

Category	Description
Type of tracer INDIVIDUAL	This individual tracer was selected from surgical patients seen on the day before the initial day of the survey.
Type of organization	Ambulatory Surgery Center (ASC)
PFAs	Assessment and Care/Services Credentialed Practitioners Information Management Medication Management
CSGs	Surgery/Anesthesia: General Surgery
Description of client selected	The 45-year-old female patient underwent a laparoscopic cholecystectomy (with intraoperative cholangiograms) and ovarian cystectomy.
Sample tracer	This tracer was conducted in the following manner: 1. The tracer began outside the building with a discussion regarding the location and signage of the building, as well as parking and security issues that the patient might have encountered. 2. The surveyor then moved to the waiting area and began a discussion with the office receptionist. The receptionist was responsible for obtaining demographic information and providing the patient with information regarding her rights and responsibilities and initial consents. The receptionist related how the patient was made aware of the potential conflict of interest in physician ownership of the ASC. The surveyor discussed issues related to patients with special needs (language, disabilities, and so forth) and responses to potentially belligerent or abusive patients. The surveyor also reviewed the receptionist's responsibilities related to recent fire and disaster drills. 3. The tracer then moved to the preoperative area. The preop nurse recounted her initial orientation and skill validation. Her ongoing competency reassessment was also discussed. She also talked about her method for obtaining information regarding advanced directives and informing the patient about the organization's policy not to honor such directives. She also reviewed her method of obtaining informed consent. For this patient, two separate consents were obtained because two distinct procedures were scheduled involving two surgeons. The nurse also reviewed the methods of performing surgical site marking while in the patient is in the preop area. 4. At this point, the tracer advanced to a separate nurse who conducted a presurgical phone evaluation several days before the scheduled surgery. The surveyor discussed issues related to screening criteria and the need for any preoperative testing required in the patient being traced. Although the patient was not a diabetic, it was discovered that diagnostic testing such as a blood glucose test or an EKG are requested individually by the anesthesiologist. However, there was no written order for such testing. 5. The tracer then moved to the operating room. The surveyor reviewed the periodic testing of equipment within the operating rooms. The circulating nurse reviewed the ASC's procedure for identifying the patient (two distinct identifiers) and demonstrated how the surgical "time out" had been performed at the time

continued on next page

Sidebar 5-2. *continued*

Category	Description
	of the surgery. The surgical scrub technician showed the surveyor how the dirty instruments from this patient's case were sterilized for future use. The technician also provided information on how the effectiveness of the sterilization equipment was documented. The surveyor also reviewed how the technician would respond to chemical agents splashing into her eyes and how she would obtain more information on the chemical agents (that is, Material Safety Data Sheets).
	In this patient's case, intraoperative cholangiograms were performed. The surveyor reviewed the system of obtaining a "wet read" from a nearby radiology group. It was discovered that official interpretations were not consistently placed in the medical record. The surveyor also noted the need to obtain credentialing documentation on such providers. The circulating nurse also reviewed the organization's system of tracking pathology specimens. The documentation did not include the surgeon's authentication of the pathology report before its inclusion in the medical record. It also identified a failure to demonstrate credentialing of pathologists providing services to this patient.
	6. The surveyor discussed the patient's care with the anesthesiologist involved. The anesthesiologist demonstrated how narcotic medications are obtained for each day's cases and followed the medication "trail" of the drugs used in the patient's case. The surveyor also reviewed the organization's "Do Not Use" abbreviation list and the response of the medical staff to its implementation as well as legibility issues. The system of making alterations to the formulary was also discussed.
	7. The tracer then moved to the postoperative area. Here, the nurse involved in the patient's care demonstrated how pain was assessed and later reevaluated and how medications were obtained, stored, and dispensed. Some of the medications used for the patient had been stored in the ASC's refrigerator. The temperature log revealed that inappropriately low temperatures were recorded without any noted action. The postanesthesia care unit (PACU) nurse also discussed how she would respond to a potential medical emergency if the patient had clinically decompensated during her care. She provided information on her specific training (ACLS) and the role she plays in checking emergency equipment each morning. The clinical alarms present in the PACU were reviewed at this time. The nurse also recounted her approach to patient education, particularly related to discharge instructions.
	8. The tracer ended at this point with documentation that the patient left the facility in the care of an adult.

Individual Tracer Example: Behavioral Health Care

Category	Description
Type of tracer INDIVIDUAL	The tracer started with a client receiving services in a behavioral health program. The surveyor was told that the client had been receiving services previously in a day treatment program operated by the same organization. The client reportedly decompensated while in the day treatment program and had to be moved to a more intensive level of care (partial hospitalization) to address her decompensation.
Type of organization	Behavioral health–provided outpatient, day treatment, and partial hospitalization services to chronically mentally ill individuals

continued on next page

Sidebar 5-2. *continued*

Category	Description
PFAs	Communication Information Management
CSGs	Partial hospitalization, day treatment
Description of client selected	Client was an adult woman, Caucasian, over 50, living in an assisted living facility (ALF) and receiving day treatment services and then partial hospitalization services at the organization in question
Sample tracer	When the surveyor found out that the client had been in day treatment, then decompensated, and was then admitted to a more intense level of care, the surveyor asked to start the tracer with the period surrounding the client's decompensation while she was in day treatment. The client received mostly group services while in day treatment. She had a psychiatrist through her ALF and was not receiving medication management services at the day treatment service provider's site. The client's group leader documented the client's deterioration over approximately a month's time in his progress notes; however, he did not indicate in his notes that he communicated this to the organization's psychiatrist, to the nurse practitioner, to the ALF's case managers, or to the client's psychiatrist. The client's group leader was not available for interview, so the surveyor reviewed the case with the psychiatric nurse practitioner who is also the clinical director. She stated that he had told her a psychiatric evaluation had been completed on this woman by the organization's psychiatric nurse practitioner within the appropriate date range. The psychiatric evaluation suggested that the woman should have her medications changed to attempt to address her anxieties and decompensation. The nurse practitioner told the woman to tell her psychiatrist to consider other medications. The nurse practitioner stated that she was empowering the woman by "leaving it in her hands." The notes in the chart suggested that the woman was not likely to take this kind of charge of herself and assert herself with her psychiatrist. The surveyor asked the nurse practitioner if she had contacted the psychiatrist or the ALF case managers and workers and made her suggestions to them. She had not. As noted previously, she justified this by saying it was the client's responsibility. The surveyor asked if that was part of their practice or expectations, that such communication occur to facilitate and coordinate care. She said it was. She was unable to provide any policies or procedures about that. The surveyor asked whether she had followed up or asked the group leader to follow up to see if the client had spoken with the psychiatrist and gotten her medications changed. She had not. The woman continued to decompensate; no changes had been made to the treatment plan. There was no indication in the record of any communication between practitioners or any attempt to head off her decompensation (other than the one psychiatric evaluation). In effect, this represents an example of probable decompensation that did not need to occur if communication had occurred between the group leader and the nurse practitioner, between the organization's providers and the providers of the ALF, and with the client (in checking to see whether she had done as she had been advised). The information was not clearly managed well in the clinical record; the treatment plan wasn't changed. The biggest problem was in the failure to plan for such communication and coordination of care to exist between the various providers of service in the organization and the ALF, especially between the psychiatrists outside the organization and those inside it.

continued on next page

Sidebar 5-2. *continued*

Individual Tracer Example: Home Care

Category	Description
Type of tracer INDIVIDUAL	Individual
Type of organization	Home health agency
PFAs	Assessment and Care/Services Communication Medication Management Information Management
CSGs	Home health Clinical/consultant pharmacy Dispensing Pharmacy
Description of patient selected	After being treated for an infection, a 64-year-old male patient was discharged from the hospital to the hospital-based home care services. The patient received home infusion services from the hospital-based pharmacy and received nursing and aide services from home health.

Sample tracer	The surveyor reviewed the clinical record in preparation for the home visit and noted that the patient was a long-term total parenteral nutrition (TPN) patient with several incidences of central line infection. Nursing visited the patient weekly to provide central line care. Some education regarding infection control was documented, but it was unclear as to who would be responsible for performing the line care. The patient's care, treatment, and services were paid for by a private insurance company; the patient had a balance of $150 each month to pay for his care. An unclean environment was noted in the safety assessment; a small child and multiple pets were present in the home as well. The patient was also taking many medications.
	
	 1. The surveyor then went on the home visit with the primary nurse, who was going to perform a central line dressing change and planned to instruct the patient/caregiver on the administration of TPN.
	
	 2. During the home visit, and based on the information found in the clinical record and discussions with the case managers, the surveyor asked the patient questions such as the following:
	   a. Can you tell me how you were informed about home care services ordered by your physician?
	   b. What kind of information did the organization provide to you when they admitted you to their services?
	   c. How did the nurse teach you about your therapy? What have you learned about special things you need to be careful about related to the TPN?
	   d. Did the nurse discuss with you how your care would be paid, since I notice that you have a balance?
	   e. How do you dispose of the needles related to your therapy? I noticed that you have pets and small children in the home; has the nurse discussed ways to help keep your home safe?

continued on next page

Sidebar 5-2. *continued*

Category	Description

> f. What instructions have you been given about what to do in an emergency, if the nurse can not get here or the electricity goes off? I see you are on a pump—do you know what to do if the power goes out?
>
> g. Can you tell me what you do if you need supplies?
>
> h. What other medications are you taking? Have you and the nurse had any discussions about the use of your medications and what they are for?
>
> i. I see that you have an aide coming out to see you. What does the aide do for you when she visits? How did you and the nurse decide what the aide would do during her visits?
>
> j. I noticed that you have used the after-hours service a few times. How was the response?
>
> k. Can you share with me the options you were given to communicate any problems you might have with the organization?

3. After visiting with the patient, the surveyor then observed the dressing change, keeping in mind some of the following infection control issues:

   a. Observed dressing change looking for infection control issues.
      1. Sterile technique
      2. Patient assessment of dressing site
      3. Hand washing
      4. Disposal of infectious waste
      5. Patient education

   The surveyor noticed that the nurse did not have a sterile change kit and "compounded" making a "sterile" field.

   As the patient had had three central line infections, the surveyor discussed with the patient the measures the patient was taught to prevent central line infection.

4. After completing his home visit with the patient, the surveyor visited the pharmacy to speak with staff about the care process for this patient. In his review of the clinical record, the surveyor noted that the patient had allergies to several medications. Based on the record and home visit indicating that the patient had an infusion pump, the surveyor noted that the pump was issued by the pharmacy; the surveyor interviewed the pharmacy technician and looked at maintenance records for the patient's pump. He also spoke with the pharmacist, asking questions such as the following:

   a. I see that Mr. Jones was admitted to home care services on July 25. What types of information did you receive about this patient before preparing the medications? What assessment information did you require?

   b. How did you prepare the medications ordered for Mr. Jones?

   c. What is your process to deliver medications to the patient?

   d. Who does the compounding of this patient's TPN? Is that something I could observe while I'm here?

   e. I noticed that Mr. Jones' pump was replaced recently. Could you explain your process for replacing pumps?

5. Back at the home health agency's office, the staff had arranged for the surveyor to meet with the patient's home health aide. The following questions were asked during the discussion:

continued on next page

Sidebar 5-2. *continued*

Category	Description
	a. How long have you been providing care to the patient? What did you do for him during your most recent visit?
	b. How did you learn about the days you were to see this patient? How was the patient aide plan of care shared with you?
	c. To whom do you report when there is a problem?
	d. I see that this patient is a DNR—how was that communicated to you?
	e. What kind of in-services have helped you prepare to care for this patient?
	f. Has your supervisor observed you giving care to this patient? What did she observe?
	g. I see that Mr. Jones has diarrhea. How do you know what personal protective equipment (PPE) you should use for this patient?
	h. I read in your notes that this patient fell one night; what did you do with that information?

Individual Tracer Example: Home Care (Hospice)

Category	Description
Type of tracer INDIVIDUAL	An individual tracer home visit with a hospice patient.
Type of organization	Hospice
PFAs	Assessment and Care/Services Communication Information Management
CSGs	Hospice in-home care
Description of patient traced	A 73-year-old female hospice patient with multiple myeloma and respiratory complications was admitted to hospice care about 30 days previously. She is also on medication for pain.
Sample tracer	Before traveling to the home to observe care of this patient by a home health aide, the surveyor looked at the patient's record to become more familiar with the patient, her care experience, and the staff involved in her care. The surveyor then traveled with a staff member to the home where the home health aide was about to make a visit. The patient was at home with her sister, who was her primary care provider.
	The surveyor noted that the clinical record indicated that the patient was unsteady on her feet and taking blood thinning medications. Before observing care, the surveyor asked the aide about the patient's care plan and what the case managers had advised her to report about the patient.
	The aide replied that she would assess the patient for such things as pain by asking, "How great is your pain?" The surveyor then asked, "How do you gauge what level of pain to report?" The aide responded that they have a policy to report any pain recorded at level 4 and above.
	Because the patient scratched a lot and had some open, bleeding sores that soiled the bed, the surveyor asked the aide about any precautions she took when changing the sheets. The surveyor then observed the home health aide changing the sheets, observing her use of PPE and infection control measures.

continued on next page

Sidebar 5-2. *continued*

Category	Description
	The surveyor then asked the sister (the care provider) about how she and her sister were educated about hospice. The sister replied that the home health nurse explained the need for hospice. Because the surveyor noted in the record that the patient had a volunteer visit each week, the surveyor asked what the volunteer had been assigned to do and whether the volunteer's visits twice a week were enough.
	The record had indicated that a social worker visited the sister to help with financial issues, so the surveyor asked the sister about the goals of the services. Chaplain services were also provided, so the surveyor noted the patient's religious background and asked the sister whether the services had been adequate. The sister also explained that the hospice had provided educational materials and educated the family on use of the oxygen unit, as delivered by the HME provider (part of the same health system). The surveyor also asked the sister if the nurse had assessed for fire safety and other environmental issues. During a review of the educational and admissions materials provided to the family, the surveyor was unable to locate a copy of a signed consent/release form. The surveyor asked how the sister and the patient had learned about their rights and what was discussed. The surveyor reviewed the record again once back in the office.
	Noting in the record that the patient's condition was worsening, the surveyor asked the sister what she had been instructed regarding when to call the hospice nurse. "We know to call hospice," she replied.
	Noticing that the aide was going to shower the patient, the surveyor asked the aide how she respects the patient's dignity and privacy.
	Noting on the record that the patient experienced early pain, the surveyor asked the sister what measures the nurse educated her on relating to pain control and verified that the medications in the home matched those in the orders.
	When the surveyor returned to the hospice office, she checked the patient's record once more to verify that a signed consent/release forms was in the record. She also asked to look at the personnel files for hospice volunteer, the chaplain, the nurse, the social worker, and the aide to verify licensure, competency, and education and training of staff. Based on the inconsistent documentation of pain assessments, the surveyor interviewed the case manager regarding the assessment process and reviewed the organization's protocols for pain management.

Individual Tracer Example: Hospital

Category	Description
Type of tracer INDIVIDUAL	Individual
Type of organization	Hospital
PFAs	Assessment and Care/services Infection Control Staffing
CSGs	Cardiac surgery

continued on next page

Sidebar 5-2. *continued*

Category	Description
Description of individual selected	A 60-year-old male admitted through the emergency department (ED) with cardiac disease. Went to cardiac cath, to the operating room (OR) for a CABG, and then to the intensive care unit (ICU). Patient had complications and ventilator-associated pneumonia.
Description of Issue of Focus or Clinical Record Selected	Primary surgical procedure at the hospital, major service line of cardiac surgery
Tracer path	ED, cardiac cath, OR, postanesthesia care unit (PACU), ICU
Sample discussion	Discussion ensued with ICU nurse, microbiology technician, respiratory therapist, ICU nurse, and intensivist. Areas of concern included the following: <ul><li>How does the ICU program evaluate and perform surveillance in postoperative patients in the ICU?</li><li>What is the staffing mix and ratio related to ventilated patients?</li><li>What is the role of microbiology in the infection control surveillance process?</li><li>What is the competence of the staff in relationship to the care of patients on ventilators?</li><li>Are there staff vacancies? Are they using traveling or agency nurses?</li><li>What is the hospital's policy on staff wearing artificial nails?</li><li>Observation of placement of alcohol-based hand wash</li><li>Observation of handwashing techniques of all staff</li></ul>

Individual Tracer Example: Long Term Care

Category	Description
Type of tracer INDIVIDUAL	Individual
Type of organization	Long term care facility
PFAs	Assessment and Care/Services Communication Infection Control Rights & Ethics
CSGs	Long term care freestanding, residents having pressure ulcers, residents having infections, residents having mobility concerns
Description of patient selected	Mrs. Jones is a 66-year-old female admitted to the facility two weeks ago after having suffered a massive CVA. She was unable to communicate verbally and was completely dependent on the staff for all her needs. She was on aspiration precautions and received thickened liquids. She had an infected Stage III pressure ulcer that was a Stage I on admission. Her family members were supportive, but they were confused and unsure about the issues related to advance directives. Although they had heard Mrs. Jones in the past express her wishes not to have her life prolonged by artificial means, they were reluctant to sign any papers.
Sample tracer	Discussion with the charge nurse: Can you tell me about the admission assessment process for Mrs. Jones? How do you assess for the risk for pressure ulcers? What do you do for those residents admitted with pressure ulcers to prevent the ulcers from getting worse?"

continued on next page

Sidebar 5-2. *continued*

Category	Description
	Response: The staff indicates they use the Braden Scale for risk assessment, which is done at the time of admission. Although Mrs. Jones' progress notes did identify the pressure ulcer on admission, progress notes revealed that the ulcer was not staged or described in depth. Although there was a form on the chart for weekly reassessments, the form was not completed. The care plan did not include basic prevention methods such as turning and repositioning and providing adequate nutrition or adequate support surfaces.
	Other follow-up activities: The organization's wound care policy does not reflect the Braden Scale assessment tool. It refers to an old assessment tool that was developed by the nursing department. The medical record review had evidence that both tools were being used and not all staff had been instructed on how to use the Braden tool. Three additional records were reviewed and revealed the lack of a completed form.
	Discussion with the nurse: What training and education have you received regarding caring for residents with pressure ulcers? Do you have a wound care nurse in the organization?
	Response: The nurse indicated that there is a wound care nurse who oversees the pressure ulcer care in the facility. She indicated that the training is provided as needed by the wound care nurse.
	Discussion with social services: Can you tell me about your discussion of advance directives with Mrs. Jones or her family? How do you follow up after initial conversations?
	Response: The social worker found a note in the record that initial information had been provided to the family. There was no indication in the record of subsequent conversations or of advance directives in progress.
	Other follow-up activities: The physician progress notes contained no information that he had spoken to the resident or family. There was no confirmation that the physician had been notified of the family's need for counseling. There were no pastoral notes on the chart.
	Discussion with the CNA: Tell me about the care you provide to Mrs. Jones. What training and education have you received to care for residents with swallowing precautions? Observations: The CNA was feeding the resident too fast and trying to give the resident liquids before the resident had swallowed any food. She did not seem to notice that Mrs. Jones had not swallowed any food. She could not explain any basic swallowing precautions.
	Follow-up activities: Review of the CNA's education file revealed that she had attended an in-service on swallowing precautions six months ago, but she had not cared for a resident with swallowing precautions since then.

The Accreditation Decision Process

The goal of the accreditation decision and reporting approach is to move organizations away from focusing on achieving high scores to achieving and maintaining safe, high-quality systems of care. The accreditation decision will be based on a simple count of the standards that are scored not compliant. The determination as to whether an organization is compliant with a given standard is based on the scoring of that standard's elements of performance (EPs.) Scoring of EPs will be on a three-point scale—satisfactory compliance (2), partial compliance (1), and insufficient compliance (0)—or not applicable (N/A). Standards will be identified as compliant or not compliant. In order to address any requirements for improvement, organizations will have a 45-day window to submit an ESC report.

Before leaving the site, the surveyor will leave an Accreditation Report of findings. In addition, the Accreditation Report will be posted on the organization's secure, password-protected extranet Web space shortly after survey. All information on the Accreditation Report will only be available to the health care organization itself or, if it is part of a system, its corporate office.

The accreditation decision categories for 2006 are as follows:

- Accredited—The organization is in compliance with all standards at the time of the on-site survey or has successfully addressed all requirements for improvement in an Evidence of Standards Compliance within 45 days following the posting of the Accreditation Report.

- Provisional Accreditation—The organization fails to successfully address all requirements for improvement in an Evidence of Standards Compliance within 45 days following the posting of the Accreditation Report.

- Conditional Accreditation—The organization is not in substantial compliance with the standards, as usually evidenced by a count of the number of standards identified as not compliant at the time of survey which is between one and a half and three standard deviations above the mean number of noncompliant standards for organizations in that accreditation program. The organization must remedy identified problem areas through preparation and submission of an Evidence of Standards Compliance and subsequently undergo an on-site, follow-up survey.

- Preliminary Denial of Accreditation— There is justification to deny accreditation to the organization as usually evidenced by a count of the number of noncompliant standards at the time of survey which is three or more standard deviations above the mean number of standards identified as not compliant for organizations in that accreditation program. The decision is subject to review and appeal prior to the determination to deny accreditation; the appeal process may also result in a decision other than Denial of Accreditation.

- Denial of Accreditation—The organization has been denied accreditation. All review and appeal opportunities have been exhausted.

- Preliminary Accreditation—The organization demonstrates compliance with selected standards in the first of two surveys conducted under the Early Survey Policy Option 1

Random Unannounced Surveys

The Joint Commission conducts random unannounced surveys on a 5% random sample of accredited organizations in each of its applicable accreditation programs to determine ongoing compliance with Joint Commission standards. An organization is eligible to receive a random unannounced survey 9 to 30 months following its full triennial survey. An organization will receive no advance notice for this type of survey.

The scope and focus of a random unannounced survey is based on both fixed and variable components. The variable components of random unannounced surveys are identified through the PFP. Presurvey information is processed through the PFP and identifies prioritized, organization-specific PFAs to be evaluated during these surveys. The presurvey information may include

Common Priority Focus Areas of 2006 Random Unannounced Surveys

Ambulatory Care

Quality Improvement Expertise/Activities
Patient Safety
Information Management

Behavioral Health Care

Assessment and Care/Service
Information Management
Patient Safety

Home Care

Assessment and Care/Service
Patient Safety
Information Management

Hospital

Assessment and Care/Service
Medication Management
Patient Safety

Long Term Care

Assessment and Care/Service
Patient Safety
Credentialed Practitioners

Results of random unannounced surveys may generate appropriate follow-up activities and can affect the organization's current accreditation decision.

Unannounced Surveys

As of January 1, 2006, the Joint Commission conducts all accreditation surveys on an unannounced basis. (See the box below for a list of exceptions to this change.) The purpose of this change is to shift health care organizations' focus away from survey preparation toward continuous standards compliance. Implementation of regular unannounced surveys reinforces the fact that the on-site survey is not the ultimate point of the accreditation process; rather, it is one component in an ongoing effort to provide safe, high-quality care, treatment, and services.

Between 2006 and 2008, the unannounced survey will occur in the year that the organization is due to have its triennial survey. Subsequent unannounced surveys will occur 18–39 months after the organization's first unannounced survey. The timing of this latter survey and all succeeding unannounced surveys will be based on pre-established criteria generated from PFP data.

previous survey findings; data from the organization's application for accreditation; and data from the Joint Commission's Quality Monitoring System, including sentinel event and complaints.

Fixed components are identified each year based on the highest PFAs and selected National Patient Safety Goals. The PFAs applicable to random unannounced surveys in ambulatory care, behavioral health care, home care, hospital, and long term care organizations in 2006 are listed in the box above. (The National Patient Safety Goals for 2006 are discussed in Chapter 2.) Both the applicable PFAs and the National Patient Safety Goals are updated each year and will be identified in *Joint Commission Perspectives*®.

This information is gathered immediately before a random unannounced survey to make sure that it is the most recent data available. The review of variable components takes precedence over the review of fixed components. The surveyor will review all variable components identified for the organization and then address fixed components as time allows.

Exceptions to Unannounced Surveys

- Initial surveys (that is, for organizations that are undergoing their first Joint Commission survey), including both surveys conducted under the Early Survey Policy

- Situations in which it would not be logical or feasible to conduct an unannounced survey, such as with the Bureau of Prisons and the Department of Defense

- Office-based surgery practices (fewer than 1,500 surgical procedures)

- Immigration facilities

- Ambulatory care organizations that provide surgery/anesthesia services (fewer than 1500 surgical procedures)

- Ambulatory care organizations that provide medical dental visits (fewer than 5,000 annual visits or less than 3 licensed independent practitioners)

- Foster care programs

- "Very small" organizations in certain situations

- Very small laboratories (fewer than 5000 tests performed annually)

- PPR option 2 and option 3 surveys

- First surveys for organizations that choose the early survey policy option

With an *unannounced survey*, a surveyed organization will receive *no notice* of its survey date before the start of the survey. In concert with the unannounced survey process, the following procedures will be implemented:

- Accredited organizations will be able to identify up to 10 days each year in which an unannounced survey should be avoided. These 10 days should not include federal holidays but may include regional events in which it may be difficult to conduct a survey during a given period. The Joint Commission will make every effort to accommodate the organization regarding avoiding these 10 days. However, the Joint Commission reserves the right to conduct a survey during an "avoid period" if the reason(s) given to avoid a survey at that time are such that a survey can be reasonably accomplished.

- An annual subscription billing model will be implemented.

- Because an accredited organization will not be able to post its survey date, and, therefore, individuals cannot request to have a Public Information Interview, a new Accreditation Participation Requirement was established. This APR requires an organization to demonstrate how it communicates to its public that if members of the public have any quality of care or safety concerns, they should notify the Joint Commission.

- On the morning of an organization's survey, the organization's PFP Summary Report, the survey agendas, and the biographies and pictures of the surveyors assigned to conduct the survey will be posted to the organization's secure site on the Joint Commission extranet site.

- If an organization knows of a surveyor who works or worked at the organization or a competing organization or has had personal experience with the survey that represents a potential conflict, the organization is asked to identify the individual(s) in its e-App.

Because of the move to unannounced surveys, effective January 1, 2006, the PPR must be updated and submitted (for applicable organizations) at one-year intervals after the organization's last survey. This modification supports a continuous accreditation process. The PPR can be used to validate or improve policies and procedures so an organization can feel confident that its systems and processes are in line with the standards and can then focus more on the delivery of safe, high-quality care to its patients.

In addition, the PFP Summary Report will be provided to accredited organizations annually. The output will also be provided to organizations at the beginning of their survey.

Index

A

Abbreviations, acronyms, and symbols (Goal 2B), 36–37, 55–56

Accreditation as risk reduction activity, 8

Accreditation decision categories
  Accredited, 69, 155
  Conditional Accreditation, 68, 69, 155
  Denial of Accreditation, 68, 155
  Preliminary Accreditation, 155
  Preliminary Denial of Accreditation, 155
  Provisional Accreditation, 68, 69, 155

Accreditation decision process, 155

Accreditation Participation Requirement (APR), 157

Accreditation process
  development of, 7
  focus of, 16, 139
  leadership role in, 16–18
  organization-specific nature of, 140

Accreditation status, 68, 69

Accreditation surveys
  on-site process, 140, 143–145
  random unannounced surveys, 155–156
  unannounced surveys, 30, 155–157

Accreditation Watch, 68

Accredited, 69, 155

Acronyms (Goal 2B), 36–37, 55–56

Action plans, 68–69

Admission to care, 46–48, 119, 120

Adverse events. *See also* Risk reduction; Sentinel events
  cardiac events, 23–24
  disclosure of, 62, 63
  medication errors, 126
  nonpunitive approach to, 10, 14
  proactive risk reduction, 12
  reduction strategies, 61
  reporting of, 10–11, 63
  staffing adequacy-related errors, 133–134
  transfusion errors, 122, 132

Alcohol-based hand rubs, 44–45, 58

Ambulatory care organizations (AMB)
  applicability matrix, 114–118
  Ethics, Rights, and Responsibilities (RI) standards
    outcomes of care (RI.2.90), 74
  Improving Organization Performance (PI) standards, 62
    data collection (PI.1.10), 75–77
    pattern and trend analysis (PI.2.20), 78–79
    proactive safety risk program (PI.3.20), 81–82
    sentinel event management processes (PI.2.30), 80
  individual tracer example, 146–147
  Leadership (LD) standards
    patient safety program implementation (LD.4.40), 83–84
    service and process design (LD.4.20), 82

Management of Human Resources (HR) standards
  continuing education and in-service training (HR.2.30), 88–89
Management of Information (IM) standards
  data collection and storage processes (IM.3.10), 92–94
  information-based decision making (IM.4.10), 94–95
  information management processes (IM.1.10), 90–91
  knowledge-based information resources (IM.5.10), 96
Management of the Environment of Care (EC) standards
  environment improvement (EC.9.30), 87–88
  environment monitoring (EC.9.10), 84–86
  environment of care issues, resolution of (EC.9.20), 86–87
medication management tracers, 127
National Patient Safety Goals, 29
  abbreviations, acronyms, and symbols (Goal 2B), 36–37, 55–56
  applicability of, 32
  critical test results, timely reporting of (Goal 2C), 37–38, 39, 56
  drug concentrations (Goal 3B), 40–41, 42, 57
  drugs, look-alike/sound-alike (Goal 3C), 41–42
  hand hygiene guidelines (CDC) compliance (Goal 7A), 43–45, 57–58
  "hand off" communication procedures (Goal 2E), 39–40
  labels on medications and solutions (Goal 3D), 42–43
  medication list on admission (Goal 8A), 46–48
  medication list on discharge or transfer (Goal 8B), 46–48
  patient identification (Goal 1A), 31–33
  read-back of orders or test results (Goal 2A), 34–36
  sentinel event from health care associated infections (Goal 7B), 45–46
  surgical fires (Goal 11), 51
  Universal Protocol for Preventing Wrong Site, Wrong Procedure, Wrong Person Surgery™, 54
  verbal or telephone orders (Goal 2A), 34–36, 57
PPR completion, 139
priority focus areas (PFAs), 156
unannounced surveys, exceptions to, 156
Ambulatory infusion services, freestanding, 97–113

O